THE
OF

THE GREAT GAIN OF GODLINESS

PRACTICAL NOTES ON
MALACHI 3:16–18

Thomas Watson

The fear of the LORD is a fountain of life (*Prov.* 14:27)

THE BANNER OF TRUTH TRUST

THE BANNER OF TRUTH TRUST
3 Murrayfield Road, Edinburgh EH12 6EL, UK
P.O. Box 621, Carlisle, PA 17013, USA

*

First published in London as
Religion Our True Interest, 1682

First Banner of Truth edition, 2006
© Banner of Truth Trust, 2006

ISBN-10: 0 85151 938 5
ISBN-13: 978 0 85151 938 8

*

Typeset in 10.5/13.5 pt Sabon at the
Banner of Truth Trust, Edinburgh
Printed in the USA by
Versa Press, Inc.,
East Peoria, IL

Contents

PART TWO

The Good Effects of Godliness

Author's Preface

CHRISTIAN READER,

Books are the children of the brain.[1] In this writing age[2] when they are brought forth *ad nauseam*, I intended that my pen should have been silent, but the variety and weightiness of this subject, as also the desire of some friends, did prevail with me to publish it.

The main design of this excellent Scripture, Malachi 3:16–18, is to encourage solid piety, and confute the atheists of the world, who imagine there is no gain in godliness. It was the speech of King Saul to his servants, 'Will the son of Jesse give every one of you fields and vineyards?' (*1 Sam.* 22:7). Will the world or men's lusts give them such noble recompenses of reward, as God bestows upon his followers? Surely, it is holiness that carries away the garland.

As for this treatise, it comes abroad in a plain dress: truth like a diamond shines brightest in its native lustre.

[1] This saying is often attributed to Jonathan Swift in 1704, but here Watson predates him by more than twenty years.

[2] 'Of making many books there is no end' (*Eccles.* 12:12).

St Paul came not to the Corinthians with excellency of speech[1] or the pride of oratory;[2] his study was not to court, but convert. It is an unhappiness that, in these luxuriant times, religion should for the most part run either into notion or ceremony; the spirits of religion are evaporated. When knowledge is turned into taste, and digested into practice, then it is saving. That God would accompany these few impolite lines with the operation and benediction of his Holy Spirit and make them edifying is the prayer of him who is

Thine in all Christian service,

THOMAS WATSON

Dowgate, London

November 1681

[1] *1 Cor.* 2:1.

[2] *Mundi facundiam non venditavit* (he did not hawk the eloquence of the world) — Johannes Vorstius, Danish theologian and philologist, 1623–76.

Publisher's Preface

This rare work by Thomas Watson has been trans-
cribed from a copy supplied by the British Library
and carefully edited. As with the other titles in this
series, the language has been slightly updated in cases
where it was felt that present-day readers might struggle
to understand the author's meaning. This updating has
been kept to a minimum, however, since Watson's heart-
searching and practical expositions are still well able to
stand on their own merits. His *Body of Divinity* was the
first title republished by the Banner of Truth in 1958 and
his works[1] have continued to be among the Trust's most
consistently useful and influential publications ever since.

The present work was first published in London in
1682 with the title *Religion Our True Interest: or
Practical Notes upon the Third Chapter of Malachy, the*

---

[1] The Trust publishes *A Body of Divinity, The Ten Commandments,*
and *The Lord's Prayer* (which together make up Watson's *Body of
Practical Divinity*, based on the Westminster Shorter Catechism),
The Beatitudes, and, in the Puritan Paperbacks series, *All Things for
Good, The Doctrine of Repentance, The Godly Man's Picture*, and
The Lord's Supper. Full details of these can be obtained from Trust
offices.

Sixteen, Seventeen and Eighteen Verses. It appears not to have been printed again until 1992 when Blue Banner Productions of Edinburgh published an edition under the original title, which is now out of print.

This Banner of Truth edition has adopted the title *The Great Gain of Godliness* from 1 Timothy 6:6 on the basis of the hint dropped by Watson in his Preface:

> The main design of this excellent Scripture is to encourage solid piety, and confute the atheists of the world, who imagine there is *no gain in godliness.*

The Trust is delighted to put into the hands of modern readers a treasure of which C. H. Spurgeon said in his *Commenting and Commentaries* (1876):

> This would be a great find if we could only come at it for Watson is one of the clearest and liveliest of Puritan authors. We fear we shall never see this commentary, for we have tried to obtain it, and tried in vain.[1]

For the present edition, some of the Latin and Greek quotations inserted in the margin by the author have been translated and put into the text and notes on the main persons referred to have been added.

May the great gain of godliness be the everlasting possession of the reader!

THE PUBLISHER
July 2006

---

[1] Interestingly, there is now a copy in the C. H. Spurgeon collection of the Curry Library, William Jewell College, Liberty, Missouri. The College acquired Spurgeon's private library containing thousands of volumes when it was put up for sale for £500 in 1905.

PART ONE

THE CHARACTER OF
THE GODLY

*Then they that feared the LORD spake often one to another:
and the LORD hearkened, and heard it, and a book of remembrance was written before him for them that feared the LORD,
and that thought upon his name*
(Mal. 3:16).

HOLDING FAST
IN EVIL DAYS

Then they that feared the LORD spake often one to another: and the LORD hearkened, and heard it, and a book of remembrance was written before him for them that feared the LORD, and that thought upon his name. And they shall be mine, saith the LORD of hosts, in that day when I make up my jewels; and I will spare them, as a man spareth his own son that serveth him (Mal. 3:16–17).

The 'scripture of truth' (*Dan.* 10:21) is the ground of faith. This portion of Scripture which now presents itself to our view has its sacred elegancies, and is *all glorious within* (see *Psa.* 45:13, AV). It was composed by Malachi, whose name means 'Messenger'. He came as an ambassador from the God of heaven. This prophet was so famous that Origen and others (though injudiciously) supposed him to be an angel. He lived after the building of the second temple, and was contemporary with Haggai and Zechariah.

This blessed prophet lifted up his voice like a trumpet and told the Jewish nation of their sins. He was the last trumpet that sounded in the Old Testament. In the words of the text are these parts:

1. A DESCRIPTION OF THE GODLY.
i. In general, they were fearers of God: *They that feared the* LORD.
ii. In particular:
    a. They spoke often one to another.
    b. They thought upon God's Name.

2. THE GOOD EFFECTS OF THEIR PIETY.
i.   The Lord regarded it: *He hearkened and heard.*
ii. He recorded it: *a book of remembrance was written.*
iii. He rewarded it; and this reward consisted in three things.
    a. God's owning them: *They shall be mine.*
    b. God's honouring them: *In that day when I make up my jewels.*
    c. God's sparing them: *I will spare them, as a man spareth his own son that serveth him.*

Before I come to the several parts distinctly, note the connective particle standing at the beginning of the text which may not be omitted, namely, the word *THEN*.

Then they that feared the LORD, etc. *Then*, that is, after Israel's return from the Babylonian captivity; *then*, when the major part of the people grew corrupt, and came out of the furnace worse than they went in (verses 13, 14),[1] in this bad juncture of time, *then they that feared the* LORD *spake often one to another*. Hence observe,

---

[1] 'There was nothing sound, either among the priests or the common people . . . they had long indulged with loose reins in all kinds of wickedness' (Calvin, *Commentary on Malachi*).

That the profaneness of the times should not slacken but heighten our zeal. The looser others are, the stricter we should be. In those degenerate times when men were arrived at the acme and height of impudence, and dared to speak treason against heaven, *then they that feared the* LORD *spake often one to another*. When others were plaintiffs these were defendants; when others spoke against God, these spoke for God.

In Noah's days all flesh had corrupted itself (the old world was drowned in sin before it was drowned in water) now at this time, *Noah was perfect in his generation, and Noah walked with God* (*Gen.* 6:9). He was the phoenix of his age. Athanasius stood up in the defence of the truth when the world was turned Arian. The more outrageous others are in sin, the more courageous we should be for truth. When the atheists said, It is vain to serve God, *then* they that feared the LORD spake often one to another.

Why should we be holiest in evil times?

1. *Because of the divine injunction.* God charges us to be singular (*Matt.* 5:47), to be circumspect (*Eph.* 5:15), to be separate from idolaters (2 *Cor.* 6:17), to shine as lights in the world (*Phil.* 2:15). He forbids us to join together with sinners, or do as they do. The way to hell is a well-trodden road, and the Lord calls to us to turn out of the road: *Thou shalt not follow a multitude to do evil* (*Exod.* 23:2). This is sufficient reason to keep ourselves pure in a time of common infection. As God's Word is our rule, so his will is our warrant.

2. *To be holiest in evil times is an indication of the truth of grace.* To profess religion when the times favour it is no great matter. Almost all will court the Gospel Queen when she is hung with jewels. But to own the ways of God when they are decried and maligned, to love a persecuted truth, this evidences a vital principle of goodness. Dead fish swim down the stream, living fish swim against it. To swim against the common stream of evil shows grace to be alive. The prophet Elijah continuing zealous for the Lord of Hosts when they had dug down God's altars (*1 Kings* 19:10, *Rom.* 11:3) showed his heart and lips had been touched with a coal from the altar.

TWO APPLICATIONS

USE 1. See hence how unworthy they are of the name of Christians who use sinful compliance, and cut the garment of their religion according to the mode and fashion of the times. They do not consult what is *best*, but what is *safest*. Complying spirits can truckle[1] to the humours of others; they can bow either to the *East* or to the *Host*; they prefer a whole skin before a pure conscience. They can, with the planet Mercury, vary their motion; they can, as the mariner, shift their sail with every wind and, as the mongrel Israelites, speak the language of Canaan *and* Ashdod. These are like the Samaritans of whom Josephus says, when the Jews flourished they pretended to be akin to them, and come of the tribe of Ephraim and Manasseh, but when the Jews were persecuted, they disclaimed kin-

---

[1] Act with servility.

dred with them. The old serpent has taught men crooked windings, and to be for that religion which does not have *truth* on its side, but *power*.

USE 2. Let us keep up the vigour of our zeal in degenerate times. We should by a holy *antiperistasis*[1] burn hotter in a frozen age. We live in the dregs of time; sin is grown common and impudent: It is excellent to walk *antipodes*[2] to the world (*Rom.* 12:2). Let us be as lilies and roses among the briars. Sin is never the better because it is in fashion, nor will this plea hold at the last day, that we did as the most. God will say, Seeing you sinned with the multitude, you shall go to hell with the multitude. Oh, let us keep pure among the dregs; let us be like fish that retain their freshness in salt waters; and as that lamp which shone in the smoking furnace (*Gen.* 15:17).

FOUR THINGS TO CONSIDER

1. To be holy in times of general defection is that with which God is greatly pleased. The Lord was much taken with the holy conferences and dialogues of these saints in the text. When others were inveighing against the Deity, that there should be a parcel of holy souls speaking of glory and the life to come, their words were music in God's ears.

2. To keep up a spirit in holiness in an adulterous generation is a Christian's honour. This was the glory of the church of Pergamum, that she held fast Christ's name,

[1] Opposition to circumstances, reaction.
[2] Diametrically opposite.

even where Satan's seat was (*Rev.* 2:13). The impiety of the times is a foil to set off grace all the more, and give it a greater lustre. Then a Christian is most lovely, when he is (as Ambrose says) like the cypress, which keeps its verdure and freshness in the winter season. *Mark the perfect man, and behold the upright* (*Psa.* 37:37). An upright man is always worth beholding, but then he is most to be admired when like a bright star he shines in the dark, and having lost all, holds fast his integrity.

3. To be good in a profligate age does much to animate weak beginners; it strengthens feeble knees (*Isa.* 35:3) and shores up those temples of the Holy Spirit which are ready to fall. One man's zeal is a burning torch for others to light at. How did the constancy of the martyrs inflame the love of many to the truth! Though only Christ's blood saves, yet the blood of martyrs may strengthen. St Paul's prison chain made converts in Nero's court, two of whom were afterwards martyrs, as history relates. Mr Bradford's holy advice and example so confirmed Bishop Ferrar that he would not touch the Roman pollution.[1]

4. How sad will it be for Christians to fall off from their former profession, and espouse a novel religion. Julian bathed himself in the blood of beasts offered in sacrifice to the heathen gods, and so as much as lay in him washed off his former baptism. In the time of Julius Caesar this astonishing thing happened: after a plentiful vintage wild grapes appeared upon their vines, which was looked upon

---

[1] Foxe, *Acts and Monuments*. Robert Ferrar, Bishop of St David's, was martyred in 1555.

as an ominous sign. When men seemed to bring forth the fruits of righteousness, and afterwards bring forth the wild grapes of impiety, it is a sad omen and prognostic of their ruin: *For it had been better for them not to have known the way of righteousness, than after they have known it to turn from the holy commandment* (2 Pet. 2:21). Let all this make us maintain the power of holiness in the worst times. Though others wonder we do not sin after the rate that they do, yet remember, it is better to go to heaven with a few than to hell in the crowd.

QUESTION: How may we keep up the briskness and fervour of grace in times of apostasy?

ANSWER 1. Let us beware of having our hearts too much linked to the world. The world damps zeal as earth chokes the fire. We are bid to *love our enemies*; but the world is such an enemy as we must not love, *Love not the world* (1 John 2:15). The world bewitches with her blandishments, and kills with her silver darts. He who is a Demas will be a Judas; a lover of the world will, for a piece of money, betray a good cause, and make shipwreck of a good conscience.

ANSWER 2. Let us be volunteers in religion; that is, *choose* God's service; *I have chosen the way of truth* (Psa. 119:30). It is one thing to be good with an end in view. Hypocrites are good only out of worldly design. They embrace the gospel for secular advantage, and these will in time fall away. The Chelidonian stone keeps its virtue no longer than it is enclosed in gold; take it out of the gold, and it loses its virtue. False hearts are good no longer than they are enclosed in golden prosperity; take them out of the gold and they lose all their seeming goodness. But if we would retain our sanctity in backsliding times we must serve God purely out of choice. He who is good out of choice loves holiness for its beauty, and adheres to the gospel, when all the jewels of preferment are pulled off.

ANSWER 3. Let us be inlaid with sincerity. If a piece of timber begin to bend, it is because it is not sound. Why do any bend and comply against their conscience, but because their hearts are not sound? *Their hearts were not right with him, neither were they steadfast* (Psa. 78:37). Sincerity causes stability. When the apostle exhorts to stand fast in the evil day, among the rest of the Christian armour, he bids them put on the girdle of truth, *Stand therefore, having your loins girt about with truth* (Eph. 6:14). The girdle of truth is nothing else but sincerity.

ANSWER 4. Let us get love to Christ. Love is a holy transport. It fires the affections, steels the courage, and carries a Christian above the love of life, and the fear of death. *Many waters cannot quench love* (Song of Sol. 8:7). Love made Christ suffer for us. If anyone ask what Christ died of, it may be answered, He died of love. If we love Christ, we will own him in the worst times, and be like that virgin of whom Basil[1] speaks who, not accepting deliverance upon sinful terms, cried out, 'Let life and money go; welcome Christ!'

---

[1] Basil (c. AD 329–379), defender of the orthodox faith against the heresies of the 4th century.

ANSWER 5. If we would keep up the sprightly vigour of grace in evil times, let us harden our hearts against the taunts and reproaches of the wicked. David was the song of the drunkards (*Psa.* 69:12). A Christian is never the worse for reproach. The stars are not the less glorious though they have ugly names given them, the *Bear*, the *Dragon*, etc. Reproaches are but *assulae crucis*, splinters of the cross. How will he endure the stake, who cannot bear a scoff? Reproaches for Christ are ensigns of honour, badges of adoption (*1 Pet.* 4:14), the high honours of accusations, says Chrysostom.[1] Let Christians bind these as a crown about their head. Better have men reproach you for being good, than have God damn you for being wicked. Be not laughed out of your religion. If a lame man laugh at you for walking upright, will you therefore limp?

ANSWER 6. If we would keep up the vigour of devotion during a general seizure, let us beg God for confirming grace. Habitual grace may flag; Peter had habitual grace, yet was foiled; he lost a single battle, though not the victory. We need exciting, assisting, corroborating grace; not only grace in us, but grace with us (*1 Cor.* 15:10); auxiliary grace (which is a fresh gale of the Spirit) will carry us undauntedly through the world's blustering storms. Thus shall we be able to keep up our heroic zeal in corrupt times, and be as Mount Zion, which cannot be moved.

---

[1] Chrysostom (AD 347–407), bishop of Constantinople.

2

THE GODLY AND
THE FEAR OF GOD

Having done with the frontispiece of the text, I begin, in the first place, with the character in general of the godly: they are fearers of God, 'They that feared the LORD'. What fear is meant here?

Considered *negatively*, it is not meant

1. of a natural fear, which is a tremor or palpitation of heart, occasioned by the approach of some imminent danger. 'Fears shall be in the way' (*Eccles.* 12:5).

2. It is not meant of a sinful fear, which is twofold:

A *superstitious* fear: a hare crossing the path is by some more dreaded than a harlot lying in the bed.

A *carnal* fear; this is the fever of the soul which sets it a shaking. 'Fear is the worst prophet in times of doubt' (Statius). He who is timorous will be treacherous; he will decoy his friend, and deny his God. Three times in one chapter Christ cautions us against the fear of men, (*Matt.* 10:26, 28, 31). Aristotle says that the reason why the chameleon turns into so many colours is through excessive fear. Fear makes men change their religion as the chameleon does her colours.

i. Carnal fear is *excruciating,* 'Fear hath torment in it' (*1 John* 4:18); the Greek word for torment is sometimes put for hell (*Matt.* 25:46). Fear has hell in it.

ii. It is *pernicious.* It indisposes for duty. The disciples, under the power of fear, were fitter to flee than to pray, (*Matt.* 26:56), and it puts men upon indirect means to save themselves: 'The fear of man bringeth a snare' (*Prov.* 29:25). What made Peter deny Christ, and Origen sprinkle incense before the idol, but fear?

Considered *positively*, the fear meant in the text is a divine fear, which is the reverencing and adoring of God's holiness, and the setting of ourselves always under his sacred inspection. The infinite distance between God and us causes this fear.

When God's glory began to shine out upon the Mount, Moses said, 'I exceedingly fear and quake' (*Heb.* 12:21). Such as approach God's presence with light feathery hearts, and worship him in a rude, careless manner, have none of this fear.

In the words are two parts.

    1. *The Act:* fear.
    2. *The Object:* the Lord.

'They that feared the Lord': the fear of God is the *sum* of all religion (*Eccles.* 12:13). Fear is the leading grace, the first seed God sows in the heart. When a Christian can say little of faith, and perhaps nothing of assurance, yet he dares not deny that he fears God (*Neh.* 1:11). God is so great that the Christian is afraid of displeasing him, and so good that he is afraid of losing him.

DOCTRINE: *It is an indispensable duty incumbent on Christians to be fearers of God.* 'Fear thou God' (*Eccles.* 5:7). 'That thou mayest fear this glorious and fearful name, THE LORD THY GOD' (*Deut.* 28:58). This goes to the very constituting of a saint. One can no more act as a Christian without fear, than he can act as a man without reason. This holy fear is the fixed temper and complexion of the soul; this fear is not *servile* but *filial*. There is a difference between *fearing God*, and *being afraid of God*; the godly fear God as a child does his father, the wicked are afraid of God as the prisoner is of the judge. This divine fear will appear admirable if you consider how it is mixed and interwoven with several of the graces.

1. The fear of God is mixed with *love* (*Psa.* 145:19, 20). The chaste spouse fears to displease her husband because she loves him: there is a necessity that fear and love should be in conjunction. Love is as the sails to make swift the soul's motion, and fear as the ballast to keep it steady in religion: love will be apt to grow wanton unless it be poised with fear.

2. The fear of God is mixed with *faith*. 'By faith Noah . . . moved with fear, prepared an ark' (*Heb.* 11:7). When the soul looks either to God's holiness, or its own sinfulness, it fears, but it is a fear mixed with faith in Christ's merits; the soul *trembles*, yet *trusts*. Like a ship which lies at anchor, though it shakes with the wind, yet it is fixed at anchor. God in great wisdom couples these two graces of faith and fear. Fear preserves seriousness, faith

preserves cheerfulness. Fear is as lead to the net, to keep a Christian from floating in presumption, and faith is as cork to the net, to keep him from sinking in despair.

3. The fear of God is mixed with *prudence:* he who fears God has the serpent's eye in the dove's head. He foresees and avoids those rocks upon which others run (*Prov.* 22:3). Though divine fear does not make a person cowardly, it makes him cautious.

4. The fear of God is mixed with *hope.* 'The eye of the LORD is upon them that fear him, upon them that hope in his mercy' (*Psa.* 33:18). One would think fear would destroy hope, but it cherishes it. Fear is to hope as the oil to the lamp, it keeps it burning: the more we fear God's justice, the more we may hope in his mercy. Indeed, such as have no fear of God do sometimes hope, but it is not 'good hope through grace' (2 *Thess.* 2:16). Sinners pretend to have the helmet of hope (1 *Thess.* 5:8), but lack the 'breastplate of righteousness' (*Eph.* 6:14).

5. The fear of God is mixed with *industry.* 'Noah . . . moved with fear, prepared an ark' (*Heb.* 11:7). There is a *fear of diffidence,* which represents God as a severe Judge. This takes the soul off from duty (*Matt.* 25:25). But there is also a *fear of diligence.* A Christian fears and prays, fears and repents. Fear quickens industry. The spouse, fearing lest the bridegroom should come before she is dressed, hastens and puts on her jewels, that she may be ready to meet him. Fear causes a watchful eye, and a

working hand. Fear banishes sloth out of its diocese. The greatest labour in religion, says holy fear, is far less than the least pain the damned feel in hell. There is no greater spur in the heavenly race than fear.

3

REASONS TO FEAR GOD

The reasons enforcing this holy fear include the following

1. *God's eye is always upon us.* He who is under the eye of his earthly prince will be careful of doing anything that would offend him: 'Doth not he see my ways, and count all my steps?' (*Job* 31:4). God sees in the dark: 'The darkness hideth not from thee' (*Psa.* 139:12). The night is no curtain, the clouds are no canopy, to hinder or intercept God's sight. He sees the heart. A judge can judge of the fact, but God judgeth of the heart (*Jer.* 17:10). He is like Ezekiel's wheels, 'full of eyes' (*Ezek.* 10:12), and as Cyril says, he is 'all eye'. Should not this make us walk with fear and circumspection? We cannot sin but our judge looks on.

2. *God interprets our not fearing him as a slighting of him.* As not to praise God is to wrong him, so not to fear God is to slight him. Of all things, a person can least endure to be slighted: 'Wherefore doth the wicked contemn God' (*Psa.* 10:13). 'To neglect us is to slight us' (Aristotle, *Rhetoric*). For a worm to slight its Maker causes the fury to rise up in God's face (*Ezek.* 38:18).

3. *God has power to destroy us:* 'Fear him which is able to destroy both soul and body in hell' (*Matt.* 10:28). God can look us into our grave, and with a breath blow us into hell, and shall we not fear him? Is it easy to wrestle with flames? 'Who knoweth the power of his anger?' (*Psa.* 90:11). What engines or buckets can quench the infernal fire? We are apt to fear men who have power in their hand to hurt us, but what is their power to God's? They threaten a prison, God threatens hell. They threaten our life, God threatens our soul, and shall we not tremble before him? Oh, how dreadful, when the great fountains of God's wrath shall be broken up, and all his bitter vials poured out! 'Can thy heart endure, or can thy hands be strong, in the days that I shall deal with thee?' (*Ezek.* 22:14).

OBJECTION: But are not we bidden to serve God without fear (*Luke* 1:74)?

ANSWER: We must not fear God with such a fear as the wicked do. They fear him as a Turkish slave does his master; they fear him in such a way as to hate him, and wish there were no God. We must not serve God with this hellish fear, but we must serve him with an ingenuous fear, sweetened with love.

4

WALKING IN THE FEAR OF GOD

The *first use* to be made of the proposition that Christians must be fearers of God is one of refutation.

It refutes the Papists who hold that a Christian cannot have assurance because he is to serve God with fear. Assurance and fear are *different* but not *contrary*. A child may have assurance of his father's love, yet a fear of offending him. Who was more fearful of sin than St Paul (*1 Cor.* 9:27)? Yet who had more assurance? 'Who loved me, and gave himself for me' (*Gal.* 2:20). Faith procures assurance (*Eph.* 1:13), fear preserves it.

The *second use* is one of instruction. Is it a duty to fear God? What strangers, then, are they to religion who are void of this holy fear! The godly fear and sin not. The wicked sin and fear not. They are like the Leviathan, who is 'made without fear' (*Job* 41:33). Lack of the fear of God is the innate cause of all wickedness: 'Whose mouth is full of cursing and bitterness, their feet are swift to shed blood' (*Rom.* 3:14–15). Why was this? 'There is no fear of God before their eyes' (verse 18). Abraham surmised that the men of Gerar would stick at no sin. Why so? 'I thought, Surely the fear of God is not in this place' (*Gen.* 20:11). The judge in the Gospel is called an *unjust judge* (*Luke* 18:6); and no wonder, for he 'feared not God' (verse 2). There must be an excess of sin where there the fear of God is lacking to restrain it. The water must overflow where there are no banks to keep it out. We live in a godless age; would men dare to sin at the rate they do if the fear of God were ruling in their hearts? Would they dare to swear, be unclean, use false weights, bear false witness, hate purity, deride God's signs in the heaven, forge plots, persecute Christ's body, if they had the fear of God before their eyes? These men proclaim to the world that they are atheists; they do not believe in the immortality of the soul. They are worse than brutish: a beast fears the fire, these fear not hell fire. They are worse than devils, for they 'believe and tremble' (*James* 2:19).

The *third use* is one of lamentation. Let us bewail the lack of the fear of God. Offended piety is leaving the earth. Why is it that so few fear God?

i. Because they have not the knowledge of God: 'They hated knowledge, and did not choose the fear of the LORD' (*Prov.* 1:29). Every sin is founded in ignorance, as the schoolmen say. If only men knew God in his immense glory, they would be swallowed up with divine amazement. When the prophet Isaiah had a glimpse of God's glory, he was struck with holy consternation: 'Woe is me! for I am undone . . . for mine eyes have seen the King, the LORD of hosts' (*Isa.* 6:5). But ignorance of God banishes fear.

ii. Men do not fear God because they presume on his mercy. God is merciful, and they do not doubt of the virtue of this sovereign balm. But who is God's mercy for? 'His mercy is on them that fear him' (*Luke* 1:50). Such as fear not God's justice shall not taste his mercy.

Let this be 'for a lamentation', that the fear of God is so vanished. Why is it almost nowhere to be found? Some fear shame, others fear danger, but where is he who fears a Deity? Diogenes[1] came into a full market with a candle and lantern. They asked him what he sought. He said, '*Hominem quæro*', 'I seek a man'; that is, a wise man. So in the crowd of people we may go and seek a man fearing God.

And not only among the generality, but even among professing Christians, how few fear God in truth! Profession is often made a cloak to cover sin. Absalom palliated his treason with a religious vow (2 *Sam.* 15:7). The Pharisees made long prayer a preface to oppression (*Matt.* 23:14). This is sordid, to carry on wicked designs *sub larva pietatis*, under a mask of piety. The snow covers many a dunghill. A snowy white profession covers many a foul heart. The sins of professors are more odious. Thistles are bad in a field, but worse in a garden. The sins of the wicked *anger* God, but the sins of professing Christians *grieve* him.

The *fourth use* is one of reproof.

i. The proposition reproves *jovial sinners*, who are so far from fearing God that they spend their time in mirth

[1] Greek philosopher, 400–325 BC.

and wantonness: 'They did eat, they drank, they married wives, they were given in marriage, until . . . the flood came and destroyed them all' (*Luke* 17:27). There is a place in Africa called Tombutium [Timbuktu], where the inhabitants spend all the day in piping and dancing. What sensual, effeminate lives do the gallants of our age live! They spend their life in a frolic, as if God had made them to be like the leviathan who plays in the sea. 'They take the timbrel and harp, and rejoice at the sound of the organ' (*Job* 21:12). They ride to hell upon the back of pleasure, and go merrily to damnation.

Though the times are sad, they have no fear in regard of the public good. Does not God call us to trembling? Our sins are the fiery comets that presage evil. May not we fear 'the glory is departing'? May not we fear the death of religion before the birth of reformation? May not we fear some portentous calamity should bring up the fear of former judgments? And (as the prophet Ezekiel says) 'Should we then make mirth?' (*Ezek.* 21:10). But jovial spirits have banished the fear of God. They 'lie upon beds of ivory, and stretch themselves upon their couches . . . drink wine in bowls, and anoint themselves with the chief ointments' (*Amos* 6:4,5). Sinners whose hearts are hardened with soft pleasures, let them have their lusts, and farewell Christ and his gospel; 'feeding themselves without fear' (*Jude* 12). But they forget death will bring in the reckoning, and they must pay the reckoning in hell. The Turkish sultan, when he intends the death of any of his *pashas*, invites them to sumptuous feast, and then causes them to be taken away from the table and strangled: so

Satan gluts men with sinful pastimes and delights, and then strangles them. Foolish gallants are like the fish that swim pleasantly through the silver streams of Jordan, till at last they fall into the Dead Sea (*1 Tim.* 6:9).

ii. It reproves *secure sinners* who have no fear of God. Like Laish of old, they are a people 'quiet and secure' (*Judg.* 18:27). Those who are least safe are most confident. Security throws men into a deep sleep. Birds that build and roost in steeples, being used to the continual ringing of bells, the noise does not at all disturb them. So sinners who have been long used to the sound of Aaron's bells, though now and then they have a peal rung out against their sins yet, being used to it, they are not startled. A secure sinner is known thus:

a. He lives as bad as the worst, yet hopes to be saved as well as the best. He does 'bless himself, saying, I shall have peace, though I walk in the imagination of my heart' (*Deut.* 29:19). As if a man should drink poison, yet not doubt but he shall have his health. A secure sinner lies in Delilah's lap, yet hopes to be in Abraham's bosom.

b. A secure sinner thinks all is well, because all is in peace. He hears others speak of a 'spirit of bondage', and the terrors they have felt for sin, yet he thanks God that he never knew what trouble of spirit meant; he thinks his conscience is good, because it is quiet. When the devil keeps the palace 'all is in peace' (*Luke* 11:21). The Philosopher [Aristotle] says, one great sign of an earthquake is excessive calmness of the air. Ungrounded peace presages an earthquake in the conscience.

c. A secure sinner is careless about the main chance, the best opportunity. The soul is the princely part, which is crowned with reason; it is 'a mirror of the Trinity', as Plato calls it. A secure sinner provides for his body, but neglects his soul; like one that waters his flowers, but never minds his jewels. Behold here a secure person, who is in a spiritual lethargy; he has no sense of the life to come; he is destitute of the fear of God.

iii. It reproves scoffers, who are the vilest of sinners: 'There shall come in the last days scoffers' (2 *Pet.* 3:3). Such were Lucian and Porphyry.[1] These Ishmaels jeer at holy walking, and make all religion a ridicule. They throw squibs of reproach at the saints. Quintinus scoffed at Christ's Apostles. In the massacre at Paris,[2] the Papists cried out to the Protestants when they murdered them, 'Where is now your God? What is become of all your Psalms now, and your prayers?'

Some martyrs in Prague, as they were at supper (being the next day to suffer) comforted themselves saying, that this was their last supper upon earth, and that tomorrow they should sup with Christ in heaven, a great Papist flouted them, saying, 'Does Christ have cooks for you in heaven?' These are devils in the likeness of men. They are far from the fear of God; the scorner's chair stands at the mouth of hell.

---

[1] Lucian of Antioch (AD 240–312) and Porphyry, the neo-Platonist philosopher (AD 232–304).

[2] On the eve of St Bartholomew's Day, 23–4 August 1572, over 30,000 French Protestants were massacred.

5

THE EXCELLENCE OF
THE FEAR OF GOD

The *fifth use* of the proposition is one of exhortation. It exhorts us to get the fear of God planted in our hearts: 'Happy is he that feareth always' (*Prov.* 28:14). The fear of God would influence all our actions. It would make us good in both tables [of God's law]. It would make us holy towards God, and righteous towards men. We would be true in our promises, just in our dealings (*Matt.* 7:12).

That I may press you to this holy fear, let me shew you the dignity and excellency of it.

1. *The fear of God is the very badge and uniform of a saint.* The saints of old were God-fearing men (*Gen.* 22:12; *Acts* 10:22); Obadiah feared the Lord greatly (*1 Kings* 18:3). All the moral virtues in their highest elevation do not make a saint, but here is his true character, he is one that fears God. St Augustine[1] said of himself that he did knock at heaven-gate *tremebunda manu*, with a trembling hand. Christ calls his elect 'his sheep' (*John*

---

[1] Augustine (AD 354–430), Bishop of Hippo in North Africa.

10:27). Sheep are of a trembling nature. The saints are tremulous, they dare not take liberties as others do.

2. *The fear of God is a main branch of wisdom.* It is called the head, 'the beginning of wisdom' (*Prov* 1:7). Wisdom is 'more precious than rubies' (*Prov* 3:15). No jewel we wear so adorns us as wisdom. Now, the fear of God is our wisdom: 'And unto man he said, the fear of the LORD, that is wisdom' (*Job* 28.28).[1]

Wherein is the fear of God the true wisdom?

i. The fear of God is wisdom in that *it makes us careful about our spiritual accounts.* Wisdom lies in nothing more than in keeping accounts exactly. The fear of God teaches a person to examine the state of his soul critically. O my soul, how is it with you? Do you gain or lose? Is your faith in its infancy, being but newly laid to the breast of a promise? Or is it grown to some stature? How is it? Does grace or sin prevail? Thus the fear of God makes us wisely balance our accounts, and see how matters stand between God and our souls. 'I commune with my own heart: and my spirit made diligent search' (*Psa.* 77:6).

ii. The fear of God is wisdom as *it makes us understand divine secrets.* 'The secret of the LORD is with them that fear him' (*Psa.* 25:14). He must be wise who is acquainted with the *arcana coeli*, the secrets of heaven. A fearer of God is acquainted with the secret of election (*1 Thess.* 1:4), of God's love (*Rev.* 1:5), of the holy unction (*1 John* 2:20). He knows God's mind: 'We have the mind of Christ (*1 Cor.* 2:16).

---

[1] 'The crown of wisdom is the fear of the Lord' (Augustine).

iii. The fear of God is wisdom in that *it makes us consider:* 'I considered my ways' (*Psa.* 119.59). A great part of wisdom lies in consideration. He who fears God considers how vain the world is, and therefore dares not love it; how short time is, and therefore dares not lose it; how precious salvation is, and therefore dares not neglect it.

iv. The fear of God is wisdom in that *it makes us walk wisely:* 'Walk in wisdom toward them that are without' (*Col.* 4:5).

a. The fear of God makes us walk *affably:* 'Abraham stood up and bowed himself to the children of Heth' (*Gen.* 23:7). Piety does not exclude courtesy.

b. The fear of God makes us walk *inoffensively:* it prevents not only scandals but indecencies: 'That I might cut off occasion from them that desire occasion' (2 *Cor.* 11:2). The veneration of a Deity causes circumcision of heart, and circumspection of life.

v. The fear of God is wisdom, as *it preserves us from hell.* It is wisdom to keep out of danger; fear makes us flee from the wrath to come.

3. *The fear of God is the best certificate to show for heaven.* Do you have knowledge? So has Satan. Do you have profession? So has Satan, he 'transforms himself into an angel of light' (2 *Cor.* 11:14). But do you have filial fear? In this you will excel him. The fear of God is, though not our plea, yet our evidence for heaven.

4. *There is that in God which may command fear:* 'With God is terrible majesty' (*Job* 37:22).

i. With God is *majesty*.

a. There is majesty in God's *Name*, Jehovah. It comes from a Hebrew root which speaks of God's absolute, eternal, and independent being.

b. There is majesty in God's *looks*. Job had but a glimpse of God, and he was even swallowed up with divine amazement: 'Now mine eye seeth thee, wherefore I abhor myself' (*Job* 42:5).

c. There is majesty in God's *words*. He speaks with majesty, as when he gave the law in thundering, insomuch that the people said, 'Let not God speak with us lest we die' (*Exod.* 20:19).

d. There is majesty in God's *attributes:* his holiness, power, justice, which are the irradiations of the divine essence.

e. There is majesty in God's *works:* 'I will speak of the glorious honour of thy majesty, and of thy wondrous works' (*Psa.* 145:5). Every creature sets forth God's majesty; we may see the majesty of God blazing in the sun, twinkling in the stars. God's majesty is discernable in those two wonders of nature, *Behemoth* and *Leviathan* (*Job* 40:18; 41:19). In short, the majesty of God is seen in humbling the children of pride. He turned King Nebuchadnezzar out to grass, and made him fellow-commoner with the beasts. Does not all this call for fear?

ii. With God is *terrible majesty*. 'He is terrible to the kings of the earth' (*Psa.* 76:12). There is a time coming when God will be dreadful to his enemies; when conscience is awake, when death strikes, when the last trump sounds. And shall we not fear this God? 'Fear ye not me?

saith the LORD: will ye not tremble at my presence?' (*Jer.* 5:22). Fearing God's justice is the way not to feel it.

And let it not seem strange to you, if I tell you, that in respect of God's infinite majesty, there will be some of this blessed fear in heaven. Not a fear that has torment in it, for perfect love will cast out fear, but a holy, sweet, reverential fear. Though God has so much beauty in him as shall cause love, and joy, in heaven, yet this beauty is mixed with so much majesty, as shall cause a veneration in glorified saints.

5. *The fear of God tends to life* (*Prov.* 19:23).

i. This is true in a *temporal* sense, 'The fear of the LORD prolongeth days' (*Prov.* 10:27); in the original it is, '*addeth* days'. Long life is promised as a blessing, 'With long life will I satisfy him' (*Psa.* 91:16). The best way to come to 'a good old age', is the fear of God. Sin curtails the life: many a man's excess wastes his vital organs, enervates his strength, and cuts him short of those years which by the course of nature might be arrived at (*Eccles.* 7:17). You that desire to live long, live in the fear of God. 'The LORD commanded us . . . to fear the LORD our God . . . that he might preserve us alive' (*Deut.* 6:24).

ii. It is true in a *spiritual* sense. 'The fear of the LORD tendeth to life': namely, to 'life eternal'. Life is sweet, and *eternal* makes it sweeter. 'Eternal life is true life' (Augustine). The life of bliss has no term of years wherein it expires: 'ever . . . with the Lord' (*1 Thess.* 4:17). The lamp of glory shines, but is not spent; so that divine fear tends to life; a life with God and angels for ever.

6. *The fear of God gives full satisfaction:* 'He that hath it, shall abide satisfied' (*Prov.* 19.23). Such as are destitute of God's fear never meet with satisfaction. 'In the fulness of his sufficiency he shall be in straits' (*Job* 20:22). This is a riddle, to be full yet not have enough. The meaning is there is still something lacking: he who fears not God, though his barns are full, yet his mind is not at rest. The sweet waters of pleasure do rather inflame the thirst than satisfy it. 'I have run through all the delights and grandeurs of the world, and could never find full contentment', said the emperor Severus. But he who has the fear of the Lord 'shall abide satisfied'.

i. He shall *be* satisfied.

His soul shall be filled with grace, his conscience with peace. A holy man said, when God had replenished him with inward joy, 'It is enough Lord, thy servant is a clay vessel and can hold no more.'

ii. He shall *abide* satisfied.

This satisfaction shall not cease; it shall be a cordial in death, and a crown after death.

7. *The fear of God makes a little to be sweet:* 'Better is little with the fear of the LORD' (*Prov.* 15:16). Why is little better? Because that little a believer has he holds *in capite*, in his Head, Christ; that little is sweetened with the love of God. He has with that little a contented mind; and contentment turns Daniel's vegetables into meat (*Dan.* 1:12). Again, that little is a pledge of more; that little oil in the cruse is but an earnest of that golden joy and bliss which the soul shall have in heaven. Thus a little with the fear of

God is better than all unsanctified riches. Lazarus's crumbs were better than the rich man's banquet.

8. *The fear of God is a Christian's safety.* He is invulnerable; nothing can hurt him. Plunder him of his money, he carries a treasure about him of which he cannot be robbed (*Isa.* 33:6). Cast him into prison, his conscience is free; kill his body, it shall rise again. He who has on this breastplate of God's fear may be shot at, but can never be shot through.

9. *The fear of God makes all things go well with us:* 'Blessed is every one that feareth the LORD . . . happy shalt thou be, and it shall be well with thee' (*Psa.* 128:1–2).
Is it not well with that man who has all things go on his side, and has nothing lacking that may do him good (*Psa.* 84:11)? If God sees health and riches good for him, he shall have them. Every providence shall centre in his happiness. Oh, what an inducement is here to solid piety! Come what times will, 'it shall be well with them that fear God' (*Eccles.* 8:12). When they die they shall go to God, and while they live everything in the world shall do them good.

10. *The fear of God is a great cleanser:* 'The fear of the LORD is clean' (*Psa.* 19:9). It is so:
i. In its own nature, it is a pure, crystal, orient grace.
ii. In the effect of it; it cleanses the heart and life. As a spring works out the mud, so it purges out the love of sin. The heart is the temple of God, and fear sweeps and cleanses this temple that it may not be defiled.

11. *The fear of God makes us accepted with God:* 'In every nation he that feareth him . . . is accepted with him' (*Acts* 10:35). What was St Paul so ambitious of? 'We labour that . . . we may be accepted with him' (2 *Cor.* 5:9). Divine fear ingratiates us into divine favour. Such as are fearless of God, neither their persons nor offerings find acceptance: 'I despise your feast days, and I will not smell in your solemn assemblies. Though ye offer me burnt offerings . . . I will not accept them' (*Amos* 5:21–22). Who will take a gift from one who has the plague?

12. *The fear of God paves the way for spiritual joy.* Some may think the fear of God breeds sadness; no, it is the inlet to joy. The fear of God is the morning star, which ushers in the sunlight of comfort: 'Walking in the fear of the Lord, and in the comfort of the Holy Ghost' (*Acts* 9:31). The fear of God has solid joy in it, though not wanton. Oecolampadius,[1] a holy man, being on his sickbed, was asked if the light offended him. He putting his hand to his heart said, *Hic sat lucis* – 'Here I have light enough.' God mixes joy with holy fear, that fear may not seem slavish.

13. *The fear of God drives out all base fear.* Carnal fear is an enemy to religion. The fear of God frightens it away; it causes courage: 'Able men, such as fear God' (*Exod.* 18:21); some translations render it, 'men of courage'. When a dictator governed in Rome, all other offices ceased. Where the fear of God rules in the heart, it expels

---

[1] Oecolampadius (1482–1531), a Protestant Reformer at Basle and Berne.

fleshly fear. When the empress Eudoxia threatened to banish Chrysostom, the preacher said, 'Tell her, I fear nothing but sin.' The fear of God swallows up all other fear, as Moses' rod swallowed up the magicians' rods.

14. *To be void of God's fear is folly:* 'I said to the fools, deal not foolishly: and to the wicked, Lift not up the horn' (*Psa.* 75:4).

i. Are not they fools who gratify their enemy? They who lack the fear of God do so. Satan baits his hook with pleasure and profit, and they swallow bait and hook and all; this pleases Satan; men's sins feast the devil. Who but a fool would humour his enemy?

ii. Is it not folly to prefer slavery before liberty? If a slave in the galley should have his freedom offered him, but should say he would rather tug at the oar and be a slave than have his liberty, would he not be judged indiscreet? Such is the case of him who fears not God. The gospel offers to free him from the miserable captivity of sin, but he chooseth rather to be a slave to his lusts. He is like a servant under the law: 'I love my master, I will not go out free' (*Exod.* 21:5). He was displeased with the year of jubilee: the foolish sinner had rather have his ear bored to the devil's service, than be translated 'into the glorious liberty of the sons of God' (*Rom.* 8:21).

iii. Is not he a fool who, having but one jewel, will venture the loss of it? The soul is the jewel, and the sinner is fearless of it, he will throw it away upon the world; as if one should throw pearls and diamonds at pear trees. Ephrem Syrus[1] used to say, 'He who pampers his body

---

[1] Ephrem Syrus (AD c. 306–c. 373), a Syrian church father and poet.

and neglects his soul, is like him who feasts his slave and starves his wife.'

iv. Is not he a fool who refuses a rich offer? If one should offer to adopt another and make him an heir of his estate, and he should refuse it, would not his discretion be called in question? God offers Christ to a sinner, and promises to entail all the riches of heaven upon him, but, lacking the fear of God, he refuses this great offer: 'Israel would none of me' (*Psa.* 81:11). Is not this a prodigy of madness? May not the devil beg every sinner for a fool at the last day.

15. *The fear of God is a sovereign antidote against apostasy.* The devil was the first apostate. How rife is this sin! More shipwrecks are on land than at sea; men make shipwreck of a good conscience. Apostates are said to put Christ to 'open shame' (*Heb.* 6:6). The fear of God is a preservative against apostasy: 'I will put my fear in their hearts, that they shall not depart from me' (*Jer.* 32:40). I will so love them that I will not depart from them; and they shall so fear me that they shall not depart from me.

16. *There are excellent promises made to them that fear God:* 'Unto you that fear my name shall the Sun of righteousness arise with healing in his wings' (*Mal.* 4:2). Here is a promise of Christ; he is a *Sun* for light and life-giving influence; and a Sun of *righteousness*, as he diffuses the golden beams of justification. And he has healing in his wings; the sun heals the air, dries up the cold moistures, exhales the vapours which would be pestilential; so Christ has 'healing in his wings'; he heals the hardness and impurity of the soul. And the horizon in which this sun

arises is in hearts fearing God: 'To you that fear my name, shall the Sun of righteousness arise.'

And there is another great promise: 'He will bless them that fear the LORD, both small and great' (*Psa.* 115:13). God blesses such in their name, estate, souls. And this blessing can never be reversed: As Isaac said, 'I have blessed him, and he shall be blessed' (*Gen.* 27:33). Such as fear God are privileged persons: none can take away from them either their birthright or their blessing.

17. *Fear is an admirable instrument in promoting salvation:* 'Work out your salvation with fear' (*Phil.* 2:12). Fear is that flaming sword which turns every way to keep sin from entering (*Prov.* 16:6). Fear stands sentinel in the soul, and is ever upon its watchtower. Fear causes circumspection: he who walks in fear treads warily. Fear gives birth to prayer, and prayer engages the help of heaven.

18. *The Lord is much pleased with such as fear him:* 'The LORD taketh pleasure in them that fear him' (*Psa.* 147:11). In the Septuagint it is, 'The Lord bears good will towards them that fear him.' Pagnin[1] and Buxtorf[2] render it, 'The LORD delights in them that fear him.' Never did a suitor take such pleasure in a person he loved as God does in them that fear him; they are his '*Hephzibah*', or chief solace (*Isa.* 62:4). He says of them as of Zion: 'This is my rest for ever: here will I dwell' (*Psa.* 132:14). A sinner is 'a vessel in which is no pleasure' (*Hos.* 8:8). But fearers of God are favourites.

---

[1] S. Pagnino of Lucca (1470–1541), philologist and Hebraist.

[2] J. Buxtorf the elder (1564–1629), professor of Hebrew at Basle.

19. *Such as fear God are the only persons that shall be saved:* 'Salvation is nigh them that fear him' (*Psa.* 85:9). Salvation is said to be 'far from the wicked' (*Psa.* 119: 155). They and salvation are so far apart that they are likely never to meet. But God's salvation is near them that fear him. What do we aspire after but salvation? It is the end of all our prayers, tears, sufferings. Salvation is the crown of our desires, the flower of our joy. And who shall be enriched with salvation, but the fearers of God? 'His salvation is nigh them that fear him.'

Let these cogent arguments persuade to the fear of God.

6

IS THE FEAR OF GOD IN OUR HEARTS?

The *sixth use* of the proposition is one of trial. Let us put ourselves upon a strict scrutiny and trial, whether we have the fear of God planted in our hearts.

QUESTION: How may we know whether we have the fear of God planted in our hearts?

ANSWER 1: *The fear of God will make a man fear sin:* 'How can I do this great wickedness, and sin against God?' (*Gen.* 39:9). Indeed, sin is the only formidable thing; this is the Gorgon's head that frightens; it is the evil of evils. It is the poison the old serpent spat into our virgin-nature: in sin there is both pollution and enmity. Sin is compared to a 'thick cloud' (*Isa.* 44:22), which not only hides the light of God's face but brings down showers of wrath. Sin is *worse than all penal evils:* there is more evil in a drop of sin, than in a sea of affliction.

i. Sin is the *cause* of affliction: it conjures up all the winds and storms in the world. Out of this viperous womb come mutinies, divisions, massacres, and the cause is worse than the effect.

ii. In affliction conscience may be quiet; the hail may beat upon the tiles when there is music in the room. But sin *terrifies the conscience*. Nero[1] in the midst of feasts and Roman sports was full of horror of mind; the numbers of men he had killed troubled him. Cataline[2] was frightened at every noise. Cain in killing Abel stabbed half the world at one blow, yet he could not kill the worm of his own conscience.

Sin is the spirits of mischief distilled, it puts a sting into death (*1 Cor.* 15:56). It is *worse than hell:*

i. Hell is a burden only to the sinner, but sin is a burden to God (*Amos* 2:13).

ii. There is justice in hell, but sin is the most unjust thing. It would rob God of his glory, Christ of his purchase, the soul of its happiness. 'It is more bitter to sin against Christ, than to suffer the torments of hell', says Chrysostom. Is not sin then to be feared? He who fears God is afraid of touching this forbidden fruit.

More particularly:

i. He who fears God is afraid to do anything that he suspects may be sinful (*Rom.* 14:23). He will not swallow oaths like pills, lest they should afterwards work in his conscience: he dares not mix anything in God's worship which he has not appointed; he fears it is like offering strange fire. Where conscience is scrupulous, it is safer to forbear; for, 'what is not of faith is sin'.

ii. He who fears God fears the appearance of sin: 'Abstain from all appearance of evil' (*1 Thess.* 5:22). Some

[1] Roman Emperor, AD 54-68.
[2] Cataline (110–62 BC) was a Roman politician.

things are *male colorata* (as Bernard says[1]); they have a bad look, and carry a show of evil in them. To go to the idol temple, though one does not join with them in worship, is an appearance of evil. He whose heart is ballasted with God's fear flies from that which looks like sin. It was a good speech of Bernard to Eugenius,[2] 'By avoiding the act of sin we preserve our peace; by avoiding the appearance of it we preserve our fame.' The fear of God makes us shun the occasion of sin: the Nazarite under the law was not only to forbear wine, but he must not eat grapes, which might occasion intemperancy. Joseph fled from his mistress' temptation; he would not be seen in her company.

The appearance of evil, though it defile not one's own conscience, may offend another's conscience: and hear what the apostle says: When you 'wound their weak conscience, ye sin against Christ' (*1 Cor.* 8:12). Such as do not avoid the appearances and inlets to sin make the truth of their grace to be suspected. How far are they from the fear of God who, forgetting their prayer, 'Lead us not into temptation', run themselves into the devil's mouth? They go to plays and masquerades, which are the lures and incentives of filthiness; others associate familiarly with the wicked, and are too often in their company: which is like going among them that have the plague; 'I wrote to you not to company with fornicators' (*1 Cor.* 5:9). Traffic is one thing, keeping company is another. Polycarp[3] would

---

[1] Bernard of Clairvaux (1090-1153), monastic reformer, mystic and theologian. Luther called him the most God-fearing monk of his time.

[2] Pope Eugenius III (1145-53).

[3] Polycarp (AD 69-155), Bishop of Smyrna and martyr.

have no society with Marcion[1] the heretic. Twisting into a cord of friendship with sinners is a show of evil; it hardens them in sin, and wounds the credit of religion.

OBJECTION: But did not Christ often converse with sinners?

ANSWER 1. Christ did sometimes go among the wicked; not that he approved of their sins, but as a physician goes among the diseased to heal them, so Christ intended to work a cure upon them (*Mark* 2:17). It was their conversion he aimed at.

2. Though Jesus Christ did sometimes converse with sinners, yet he could receive no infection by them; his divine nature was a sufficient antidote against the contagion of sin. As the sun cannot be defiled with the thick vapours which are exhaled from the earth, and fly into the middle region, so the black vapours of sin could not defile the Sun of righteousness. Christ was of such spotless purity that he had no receptibility of evil. But the case is otherwise with us; we have a stock of corruption within. Therefore it is dangerous to incorporate with the wicked, lest we be defiled.

Such as revere the divine majesty dare not go near the borders of sin. Those who went near the fiery furnace, though they did not go into it, were burned (*Dan.* 3:22). A wise Christian should in all his transactions put those three questions of Bernard to himself, Whether is this I do lawful, or decent, or expedient?

[1] Marcion (d. AD 160), rejected all the Old and most of the New Testament Scriptures.

iii. He who fears God, dares not sin secretly. A hypo-crite may forbear gross sin because of the shame, but not clandestine secret sin. He is like one that shuts up his shop windows, but follows his trade within doors. But a man fearing God dares not sin, though he had Gyge's ring[1] and could walk invisibly, and no eye see him. 'Thou shalt not curse the deaf, or put a stumbling block before the blind; but shalt fear thy God' (*Lev.* 19:14). If one should curse a deaf man, he cannot hear him; or lay a stumbling block in a blind man's way, he cannot see him. Yes, but the fear of God will make one avoid those sins which can neither be heard or seen by men. God's seeing in secret is sufficient *supersedeas*[2] and counter-poison against sin.

iv. He who fears God dares not commit sin, though it might bring him a profitable advantage. Gain is the golden bait with which Satan fishes for souls. This was the last temptation the devil used to Christ: 'All this will I give thee' (*Matt.* 4:9). How many bow down to the golden image! Joshua who could stop the course of the sun, could not stop Achan in his pursuit after the wedge of gold. But he who fears God dares not sin to get prefer-ment: David dared not touch the Lord's anointed, though he knew he was to reign next (*1 Sam.* 26:23). A godly man is assured that a full purse is but a poor recompense for a wounded conscience. If any shall go to choke him with steeples, he says with Peter: 'Thy money perish with thee' (*Acts* 8:20).

---

[1] King of Lydia (c. 685–57 BC). According to legend, he won his position by means of a magic ring of invisibility.

[2] *Supersedeas:* a writ to stay proceedings.

v. He who fears God, dares not gratify his own revengeful humour. Homer says that revenge is sweet as dropping honey; but grace makes a man rather bury an injury than revenge it. He knows who has said, 'Vengeance is mine, I will repay' (*Rom.* 12:19). He who has the fear of God before his eyes, is so far from revenge that he requites good for evil. Miriam murmured against Moses, and Moses prayed for her, that God would heal her of her leprosy (*Num.* 12:13). The prophet Elisha, instead of smiting his enemies, 'set bread and water before them' (2 *Kings* 6:22).

vi. He who fears God dares not do that which is of evil report, though possibly the thing in itself may be no sin. 'Dare any of you having a matter against another, go to law before the unjust?' (*1 Cor.* 6:1). Yes, some might say, what sin is it to have a just cause brought before unbelievers, that it may be decided? Oh but, might the apostle reply, though the thing in itself be lawful, yet because it sounds evil, and exposes your religion to the scorn and insult of unbelievers, you that fear God should not dare to do it. It were better to decide it by a prudent arbitration. 'All things are lawful unto me, but all things are not expedient' (*1 Cor.* 6:12).

vii. He who fears God is not only afraid of evil actions, but to offend God in his thoughts: 'Beware that there be not a thought in thy wicked heart', etc. (*Deut.* 15:9). To think of sin with delight is to act it over in the imagination. This is culpable. A man may think himself into hell. What were the apostate angels damned for, was it for any more than proud thoughts?

This is the first note of trial: He who reverences a Deity flees from sin. It is a saying of Anselm,[1] 'If sin were on one side and hell on the other, I would rather leap into hell than willingly sin against God.'

ANSWER 2: *He who fears God walks by rule rather than example.* Example is, for the most part, corrupt. Examples of great men are influential. Pharaoh had taught Joseph to swear, but Joseph had not taught Pharaoh to pray. The examples of others cannot justify a thing intrinsically evil. A God-fearer directs the rudder of his life according to the compass of the Word. He looks to the sacred canon as the mariner to the lodestar, or Israel to the pillar of fire, to direct him. 'To the law and to the testimony' (*Isa.* 8:20).

ANSWER 3: *He who fears God keeps his commandments:* 'Fear God and keep his commandments' (*Eccles.* 12:13). Luther said he had rather obey God than work miracles. A gracious soul crosses his own will to fulfil God's. If the Lord bid him crucify his favourite sin or forgive his enemies, then he instantly obeys. A heathen exercising much cruelty to a Christian, asked him in scorn what great miracle his master Christ ever did? The Christian replied, 'This miracle, that though you use me thus cruelly, I can forgive you.' A holy heart knows there is nothing lost by obedience. David swore to the Lord that he would not rest till he found a place for God (*Psa.* 132:4–5). And God swore again to David that of the fruit of his body he would set one upon his throne (*Psa.* 132:11).

---

[1] Anselm of Canterbury (1033–1109), philosopher and theologian.

ANSWER 4: *He who fears God is alike good in all companies*. He diffuses the sweet savour of godliness wherever he goes. Hypocrites can change themselves into all shapes and be as their company is; serious in one company and vain in another. He who reverences a Deity, is *semper idem*, alike good in all places. A steady pulse shows health: a steady walk shows grace. If a good man be providentially placed among the wicked, he will not coalesce with them, but in his deportment displays a majesty of holiness.

ANSWER 5: *He who fears God is good in the position where God has set him*. Take an instance in Joseph: 'I fear God' (*Gen.* 42:18). And see a pattern of relative sanctity: he showed towards his master fidelity, towards his mistress purity, towards his father duty, towards his brethren generosity. A good man makes his family *palaestra pietatis*, a training ground of piety (*Psa.* 102:1), as it was said of Cranmer.[1]

ANSWER 6: *He who fears God, dares not neglect family or closet prayer*: 'I give myself unto prayer' (*Psa.* 109:4). Prayer whispers in God's ears. Clemens Alexandrinus[2] calls it 'private conference with God'. Why was Nymphas' house called a church (*Col.* 4:15), but because it was consecrated by prayer? A gracious soul puts forth fervent sighs in prayer (*Rom.* 8:26). And surely that prayer soonest pierces heaven which pierces one's own heart.

[1] Thomas Cranmer (1489–1556), Archbishop of Canterbury, Reformer and martyr.
[2] Clement of Alexandria (c. AD 150–c. 220), early Christian apologist and theologian.

If prayer be made the touchstone, then the number of those who fear God is but small. Are there not many prayerless families in this city and nation? 'Thou casteth off fear, thou restraineth prayer' (*Job* 15:4). When men restrain prayer, they cast off the fear of God. It is the brand set upon reprobates: they 'call not upon the LORD' (*Psa.* 14:4).

ANSWER 7: *He who fears God will not oppress his neighbour:* 'Ye shall not oppress one another; but thou shalt fear thy God' (*Lev.* 25:17). How can he be holy who is not just? A saint, yet an extortioner, is a solecism. A cruel oppressor is like Judas, his bowels are fallen out. The fear of God would cure this. 'Will ye even sell your brethren? . . . Ought ye not to walk in the fear of our God?' (*Neh.* 5:8–9). As if Nehemiah had said, If you had the fear of God you would not be so wicked, you would not rise upon the ruins of others and, to wrong them, damn yourselves.

ANSWER 8: *He who fears God is given to works of mercy.* The fear of God is always joined with love to our brethren. Grace may have a trembling hand, but it does not have a withered hand; it stretches itself out to relieve the needy: 'Pure religion and undefiled before God and the Father is this, To visit the fatherless and widows in their affliction' (*James* 1:27). To visit them is not only to go to see them in affliction. Our Saviour expounds what visiting is in Matthew 25:36: 'Ye visited me'; how was that? 'I was an hungred, and ye gave me meat' (verse 35). Good works are not the cause of our justification, but they are the evidence. How far are they from the fear of God who are hard-hearted to Christ's poor! You may as well extract oil out of a flint as the golden oil of charity out of their hearts. The rich man denied Lazarus a crumb of bread, and he was denied a drop of water (*Luke* 16:21).

ANSWER 9: *He who fears God would rather displease man than God*: 'The midwives feared God, and did not as the king of Egypt commanded them, but saved the men children alive' (*Exod.* 1:17). What, not obey the king's command! How could this stand with their allegiance? Very well, because it was an unlawful command. The king had them put to death the males of the Hebrews, which they dared not do, for fear of incurring God's displeasure. King Nebuchadnezzar erected a golden image to be worshipped, but the three children (or rather champions) said, 'Be it known unto thee, O king, that we will not serve thy gods nor worship the golden image which thou hast set up' (*Dan.* 3:18). They would rather burn than bow. He who fears God knows it is best to keep in with God; he is the surest Friend, but the sorest Enemy.

ANSWER 10: *The fear of God will make a man fear these six things:*

   i. Satan's snares
  ii. His own heart
 iii. Death
  iv. Judgment
   v. Hell
  vi. Heaven

i. The fear of God will make a man afraid of *Satan's snares*. He has the eye of faith to see these snares, and the wing of fear to fly from them. *Pedibus timor addidit alas* (fear gives wings to the feet). 'We are not ignorant of his *devices*' (2 *Cor.* 2:11). The word means 'subtle strata-gems'. Satan is called the 'old Serpent' (*Rev.* 12:9). Though he has lost his holiness, he has not lost his policy: his snares are so cunningly laid, that without the guidance of God's fear we cannot escape them.

a. One subtle artifice of Satan is to bait his hook with religion. He can change his flag, and hang out Christ's colours; here he transforms himself into an angel of light (2 *Cor.* 11:14). The devil tempts men to evil, 'that good may come' of it (*Rom.* 3:8). He whistles them into the snare of preferment, that hereby they may be in a capac-ity of doing God more service. The white devil is worst. Who would suspect Satan when he comes as a divine and, if need be, can quote Scripture?

b. Another snare of Satan is to tempt to sin under a plea of necessity. Lot offered to expose his daughters to the lusts of the Sodomites that he might preserve his angel-guests who were come into his house (*Gen.* 19:8). Did not Satan instigate him to this? Necessity will not excuse impiety.

c. It is a snare to colour over sin with the pretence of vir-tue. Alcibiades[1] hung a curtain curiously embroidered over a foul picture full of owls and satyrs. Satan puts good names on sin, as physicians call that film in the eye which hinders the sight a 'pearl' in the eye. Satan coloured

---

[1] Alcibiades (450–404 BC), Athenian politician and general.

over Jehu's ambition with the name of zeal (2 *Kings* 10:16). He makes men believe revenge is valour, covetousness frugality; as if one should write 'tonic-water' upon a glass of poison.

d. Another snare of Satan is to carry on his mischievous designs under a pretence of friendship. He puts off his lion's skin, and comes in sheep's clothing. Thus Satan came to Christ: 'Command that these stones be made bread' (*Matt* 4:3). As if he had said, 'I see you are hungry; I therefore out of pity counsel you to get something to eat, turn stones to bread that your hunger may be satisfied.' But Christ spied the serpent in the temptation and repulsed him. Thus Satan came to Eve in the guise of a friend. He said of the tree in the midst of the garden, 'Ye shall not surely die . . . ye shall be as gods' (*Gen.* 3:4–5). As if to say, 'I persuade you only to that which will put you into a better condition than now you are; eat of the tree of knowledge and it will make you omniscient.' What a kind devil was here! But Eve found a worm in the apple. *Timeo Danaos et dona ferentes.*[1]

e. A fifth snare: if Satan cannot take a Christian off from duty, he will put him on too far in duty. Humiliation is a duty, but Satan suggests that the soul is not humbled enough: and indeed he never thinks it humbled enough till it despairs. Satan comes thus to a man: 'Your sins have been great, and your sorrow should be proportionable. But is it so? Can you say you have been as great a mourner as you have been a sinner? What is a drop of sorrow

---

[1] I fear the Greeks bearing gifts (Virgil's *Aeneid*). Said by Laocoon concerning the Trojan horse.

to a sea of sin?' This is laid only as a snare. The subtle enemy would have a Christian weep himself blind, and in a desperate humour throw away the anchor of hope. And if Satan has such fallacies, and as a decoy draws so many millions into his snares, is there not cause of jealous fear lest we should be trapped? The fear of God will make us fear hell's stratagems. Satan's snares are worse than his darts.

ii. The fear of God will make a man afraid of *his own heart*. Luther used to say he feared his own heart more than the Pope or cardinals. 'The heart is deceitful above all things' (*Jer.* 17:9).

It is *'deceitful'*. The word signifies, it is a 'Jacob' or 'supplanter'. As Jacob supplanted his brother, and took away the blessing, so our hearts would supplant and beguile us. *'Above all things'*: there is deceit in weights, deceit in friends; but the heart has an art of deceiving beyond all. In the best hearts there is some fallaciousness. David was upright in all things, 'save only in the matter of Uriah' (*1 Kings* 15:5). A godly man, knowing there is a spice of this deceit in his heart, fears himself. The flesh is a bosom-traitor. No man can believe what evil is in his heart. 'Is thy servant a dog?' (*2 Kings* 8:13). Hazael could not believe his heart could give birth to such monsters. If one had come to Noah and said, 'You will be drunk shortly'; he would have said, 'Is thy servant a dog?' No man knows what is in his breast, or what scandal he may fall into if God should leave him. Christ warns his own apostles to 'take heed of surfeiting and drunkenness' (*Luke* 21:34). A godly man therefore fears his heart with a fear of caution and jealousy. The heart is not only stubborn, but subtle. Let us a little trace this impostor, and see if there is not cause to fear it. The heart shows its deceitfulness regarding *things sinful* and *things sacred*.

Regarding things sinful, this deceit is in the hiding of sin, as Rahab hid the spies in the flax (*Josh*. 2:6). So the heart hides sin. And how does it hide sin? Just as Adam hid himself under fig leaves, so the heart hides sin under the fig leaves of excuses. It was done against the will, or in a passion; or it was done along with others. Aaron laid his sin in the making of the golden calf upon the people: 'The people are set on mischief' (*Exod*. 32:22). And Adam tacitly laid his sin upon God himself: 'The woman whom thou gavest to be with me, she gave me of the tree' (*Gen*. 3:12), as if to say, 'If you had not given me this tempting woman, I would not have eaten.'

The heart's deceit is seen in flattering us. It will make us believe we are not so bad as we are. The Physician deceives the patient when he tells him his disease is not so dangerous, when he is falling into the hands of death. The heart will tell a man he is free from theft, when yet he robs others of their good name; he is free from drunkenness when, though he will not be drunk with wine, he will be drunk with passion. Thus the heart is a flattering mirror to make one look fairer than he is; and is there not cause to suspect this impostor?

Secondly, the heart shows its deceitfulness regarding *things sacred*; it will be ready to put us off with counterfeit grace. Many have been deceived in taking false money, and many, it is to be feared, in taking false grace.

The heart is ready to deceive with a false *repentance*. A sinner is troubled a little for sin, or rather the consequences of it, and perhaps sheds a few tears, and now his heart soothes him up that he is a true penitent. But every legal terror is not repentance: 'They were pricked in their hearts' (*Acts* 2:37); yet after this, 'Peter said unto them repent' (verse 38). If every slight trouble for sin were true repentance, then Judas and Cain may be lifted into the number of penitents. Evangelical repentance works a change of heart (*1 Cor.* 6:11). It produces sanctity. But the false penitent, though he has trouble of spirit, yet has no transformation or change. He has a weeping eye, but an adulterous heart. Ahab fasts and puts on sackcloth, but after this, he puts the prophet Micah in prison (*1 Kings* 22:27).

The heart is apt to deceive with a false *faith;* it would put the dead child in the place of the living. Those in the second chapter of John are said to believe; but Christ did not believe their faith (*John* 2:24). True faith, as it casts itself into Christ's arms to embrace him, so it casts itself at Christ's feet to serve him; but spurious faith, though it is forward to receive Christ's benefits, yet it plucks the government from his shoulders (*Isa.* 9:6). It would have him a priest, but not upon his throne (*Zech.* 6:13). Thus the heart is full of fallacies; he who fears God fears his heart lest it should rob him of the blessing. That saying of Epicharmus[1] is good, 'Remember not to trust.'

iii. The fear of God will make a man fear *death*. Death may challenge a part in our fear, first, because it is such a

---

[1] Epicharmus (540–450 BC), Sicilian father of Greek comedy.

serious thing, it is the inlet to eternity and puts us into an unalterable estate. Secondly, because of its proximity. It is nearer to us than we are aware; it may be within a few hours march of us. God may this night seal a lease of ejectment, and say, 'Give an account of your stewardship'; and what if death should come before we are ready? Thirdly, because after death there is nothing to be done for our souls, there is no repenting in the grave: 'There is no work, nor device . . . in the grave, whither thou goest' (*Eccles.* 9:10). So death is to be feared with a holy and religious fear.

QUESTION: How far may a child of God fear death?

ANSWER 1: So far as the fear of death is a curb bit to keep him from sin. A believer may lawfully make use of all means to deter him from sin. There is no stronger antidote against sin, says Augustine, than the fear of death. Am I sinning, and tomorrow may be dying?

ANSWER 2: A child of God may so far fear death, as it makes him die to the world. The fear of death would sound a retreat and call us off from vanity. What is the world? We must leave it shortly, and all we can purchase is a burying place (*Gen.* 49:30).

ANSWER 3: A child of God may so far fear death as this fear fits him more for death. Jacob feared his brother Esau's coming against him, and he prepared to meet him, addressing himself to prayer (*Gen.* 32:7, 24). So when we fear death's coming and we prepare to meet it, we set our soul in order. This is a good fear of death.

But this fear of death in the godly must be mixed with hope. The nature of death to a believer is quite changed:

death is in itself a curse, but God has turned this curse into a blessing. To a child of God, death is not a destruction but a deliverance. When the mantle of his flesh drops off, he ascends in a fiery chariot to heaven.

iv. The fear of God will make a man fear *judgment*. Anselm spent most of his thoughts upon the Day of Judgment; and Jerome thought he always heard that voice sounding in his ears, *Surgite mortui*, 'Arise ye dead, and come to judgment'. That there shall be such a day is evident:

a. From God's *veracity:* he who is the Oracle of truth has asserted it: 'For he cometh, for he cometh to judge the earth' (*Psa.* 96:13). There is duplication here, firstly, to show the certainty: 'he cometh, he cometh'. It is an indubitable maxim. Secondly, to show the speediness, 'he cometh, he cometh', the time draws near, it is almost daybreak, and the judge is ready to take the bench (*James* 5:9). God's decree cannot be reversed.

b. There shall be such a day for the vindication of God's *justice*. Things seem to be carried in the world partially: the godly suffer, the wicked prosper. Atheists are ready to think God has thrown aside the government of the world, and does not mind how things are transacted here below. Therefore there must be a judicial process, that God may undeceive the world and set things right.

c. That there shall be such a day is evident by the principles engrafted in a natural *conscience*. When Paul reasoned of judgment to come, 'Felix trembled' (*Acts* 24:25). The prisoner at the bar made the judge tremble. That a wicked man dying is so surprised with terrors, from where does this arise but from a secret apprehension of judgment ensuing?

It will be a great Assize. Never was the like seen: 'We must all appear before the judgement seat' (2 *Cor.* 5:10). There is no flying, no absconding, no bribing, no appearing by a proxy, but all must make their personal appearance. They who were above trial here, and the law could not reach them, must appear before the tribunal of heaven.

Who shall be the Judge? Jesus Christ (*John* 5:22; *Acts* 17:31). 'He hath appointed a day, in the which he will judge the world . . . by that man whom he hath ordained.' From the fact that Christ is called a man, the Socinians blasphemously deny the essential deity of Christ. That he is God is most clearly evinced from Isaiah 9:6; John 1.1; 1 Corinthians 8:6; 1 John 5:20. 'We are in him that is true, even in his Son Jesus Christ. This is the true God.' Christ is 'consubstantiate' with God the Father (*Heb.* 1:3). But Christ the Judge is called man because he shall judge the world in a visible shape. He must be both God and man: he must be God that he may see men's hearts and he must be man that he himself may be seen.

What a solemn day will this be, when Christ shall sit upon the bench of judicature! He will judge 'righteously' (*Psa.* 9:8). Though he himself was wronged, he will do no wrong. And he will judge critically: 'Whose fan is in his hand and he will throughly purge his floor' (*Matt.* 3:12). He will see what is wheat and what is chaff, who have his image upon them and who the mark of the beast. Surely the fear of God will cause a holy trembling at the thoughts of this day.

QUESTION: In what sense should those that fear God fear the Day of Judgment?

ANSWER: Not with a fear of amazement or despondency, for the Day of Judgment will be a Jubilee, a blessed comfortable day to them. The thrush sings at the approach of rain and so may believers at the approach of Judgment. Christ who is their Judge is also their Advocate. But,

a. The godly should so fear judgment as every day to renew their sorrow for sin. They have sins *quotidiani incursus*, that creep upon them daily, and they must with Peter weep bitterly: they must steep their souls in the salty tears of repentance. It would be sad to be found at the last day in any sin unrepented of.

b. The godly should so fear the Day of Judgment as to make them afraid of sins of omission. Not dressing a wound brings death. Not discharging duty may bring damnation. You may read the solemn process at the last day: 'I was an hungred and ye gave me no meat, naked and ye clothed me not, sick and in prison and ye visited me not' (*Matt.* 25:42). The charge here brought in is for sins of omission. Christ does not say, 'You took away my meat from me', but 'You gave me no meat'; He does not say, 'You put me in prison', but 'You did not visit me.' The sins of omission condemned them. Not praying in the family, not sanctifying the Sabbath, not giving alms, will be the fatal indictment.

c. The godly should so far fear the Day of Judgment as to make them afraid of dissembling in religion. For at that day false hearts will be unmasked. Why did Paul walk with such integrity? 'Ye are witnesses and God also, how holily, and justly, and unblameably we behaved ourselves among you' (*1 Thess.* 2:10). What was the cause of this? Surely a fear of the Judgment Day approaching: 'For we must all appear before the judgement seat of Christ' (*2 Cor.* 5:10). The word in the original means we must be made manifest, our hearts must be laid open before men and angels. Such is the witchcraft of hypocrisy that it is hard in this life to know who is false and who is sincere; but shortly there will be a full discovery. It is good for God's people so to fear judgment as to make them strive against prevarication and hypocrisy; for then the hypocrite will be found out.

v. The fear of God makes a man fear *hell*. Hell is called the 'place of torment' (*Luke* 16:28). Not only notoriously wicked sinners, but such as fear God, ought to fear hell: 'I say unto you my friends, Fear him who hath power to cast into hell' (*Luke* 12:4).

QUESTION: How far should God's people fear hell?

ANSWER: Not so as to let go their hope. A mariner fears a storm, but not so as to throw away his anchor. Such as fear God should fear hell in four ways.

a. They should fear hell *tanquam meritum*, as that which they have deserved. Their sins have merited hell. Woe to the holiest man alive if God should weigh him in the balance of his justice.

b. Those who fear God ought to fear hell insofar as this is a means to make them shake off spiritual sloth. This disease is apt to seize upon God's own people; the 'wise virgins slumbered' (*Matt.* 25:5). Now, so far as the fear of hell is an alarm or a watch bell to awaken the godly out of security and make them run faster to heaven, so far it is a good and blessed fear.

c. The fear of hell is good in the godly insofar as it makes them afraid of being in the number of those who shall go to hell. There are certain persons in danger of hell:

First, those who have their heaven in this life: 'Thou that art given to pleasure' (*Isa.* 47:8). Epicures swim in sensual delights; they would rather displease God than deny the flesh. These shall take up their quarters in hell. 'In that day did the Lord GOD of Hosts call to weeping . . . and behold joy and gladness . . . eating flesh, and drinking wine . . . surely this iniquity shall not be purged from you till ye die, saith the Lord GOD of hosts' (*Isa.* 22:12–14); that is, this sin shall not be done away by any sacrifice.

Second, they are in danger to be cast into hell who live in the sin of adultery (*Prov.* 22:12); they who burn in lust shall burn in hell: 'The Lord knows how to reserve the unjust to be punished': 'but chiefly them that walk after the flesh, in the lust of uncleanness' (2 *Pet.* 2:9–10).

See the corruption of man's nature! If God had made all common, man would have sought an enclosure; and now that God has made an enclosure, man endeavours to lay all common. Instead of drinking water out of his own cistern, he loves stolen waters (*Prov.* 9:17). The same Latin word *præsepe* signifies a stable, and a whore-house: both are for beasts.

Third, they are likely to go to hell who, by giving bad example, cause others to sin. Bad example, like the plague, is catching. Great men are mirrors by which the common people dress themselves. Such as give bad example have not only their own sins but the sins of others to answer for. That doubtless was the reason why the rich man entreated Abraham that one might go from the dead to preach to his brethren (*Luke* 16:27), not that he had love to their souls, but because, while he was alive, he had occasioned his brethren's sins by his wicked example and knew that their coming to hell would increase his torment.

Fourth, they are likely to go to hell who live and die in the contempt of God's Word. Ministers have preached till the bellows are burnt, their vitals wasted, but men stop their ears and harden their hearts: 'They made their hearts as an adamant stone' (*Zech.* 7:12). Hardness of heart lies in the insensibility of the conscience (*Eph.* 4:19), and the inflexibility of the will (*Jer.* 44:16–17). Obdurate sinners shake out the arrow of conviction and scorn reproof. When the prophet cried to the altar of stone it broke apart (*1 Kings* 13:2), but sinners hearts do not break; these are likely to have the wrath of God flame about their ears: 'The Lord Jesus shall be revealed from heaven . . . in flaming fire taking vengeance on them . . . that obey not the gospel' (*2 Thess.* 1:7–8).

Fifth, they shall go to hell who fall away finally (*Matt.* 13:6). Because they had no root they withered. Flowers in a waterpot will keep green and fresh a while, but having no root wither. Demas and Julian made a fair show a while, but ended as the silkworm which, after all her curious spinning, at last becomes a common fly. 'If we sin wilfully after that we have received the knowledge of the truth, there remaineth no more sacrifice for sins' (*Heb.* 10:26). Thus we see who are likely to be thrown into hell. Now it is good for the godly so to fear hell as to fear to be in the number of those who shall go to hell.

d. The fear of hell is good in the godly insofar as it is a fear mixed with rejoicing: 'Rejoice with trembling' (*Psa* 2:11). A believer's fear of hell must be like the fear of the two Marys going from the sepulchre: 'They departed from the sepulchre with fear and great joy' (*Matt.* 28:8): fear, because they had seen an angel; and joy, because Christ was risen. So must the godly look on hell, with fear and joy: fear, because of the fire; joy, because Christ has freed them from it. A man that stands upon a high rock, fears when he looks down into the sea, yet rejoices that he is not there struggling with the waves. So a child of God, when he looks down into hell by contemplation, may fear because of the dreadfulness of the torment; yet this fear should be mingled with joy, to think he shall never come there. Jesus has delivered him 'from the wrath to come' (*1 Thess.* 1:10).

vi. The fear of God will make a man fear *heaven*. You may say, that is strange; rather hope for heaven. No, a regenerate person is to fear heaven lest he fall short of it. 'Let us therefore fear, lest, a promise being left us of enter-ing into his rest, any of you should seem to come short of it' (*Heb.* 4:1). It is a metaphor taken from athletes who, growing weary and lagging behind, come short of the prize. Who had more hope of heaven than St Paul? Yet he was not without his fears: 'I keep under my body . . . lest . . . when I have preached to others, I myself should be a castaway' (*1 Cor.* 9:27). And well may he who shall go to heaven fear least he miss it, if you consider:

a. It is possible for many who make a splendid profession to lose heaven. What do you think of the foolish virgins? They are called virgins because they were not tainted with any gross sin; yet these virgin-professors were shut out (*Matt.* 25:10). Balaam, a prophet, Judas an apostle, were both dismissed. We have seen some ships which had glorious names given them, the *Good-speed*, the *Hope*, the *Safeguard*, lost at sea.

b. It is possible to come near to heaven, yet fall short of it: 'Thou art not far from the kingdom of God' (*Mark* 12:34); yet he was not near enough. Men may countenance the ministry of the Word, have their affections moved at an ordinance, and in outward show out-go the children of God (*Num.* 23:1–2); yet, not having the oil of sincerity in their vessels, they may be frustrated of happiness. And how dismal is that, to lose God, to lose their souls, to lose their hopes! The millions of tears shed in hell are not sufficient to bewail the loss of heaven. Well may such as have heaven in them fear their coming short of it.

So much, then, for this *sixth use*, trial.

QUESTION: How shall we arrive at this blessed fear?

ANSWER 1. Let us set God ever in our eye, study his immensity. He is God Almighty (*Gen.* 17:1). He gives laws to the angels, binds the consciences of men, cuts off the spirit of princes (*Psa.* 76:12). The thoughts of God's incomprehensible greatness would strike a holy awe into our hearts. Elijah wrapped his face in a mantle when God's glory passed by. The reason men do not fear God is because they entertain slight thoughts of him: 'Thou thoughtest that I was altogether such an one as thyself' (*Psa.* 50:21).

2. Let us pray for this fear of God, which is the root of all holiness, and the mother of all wisdom: 'Unite my heart to fear thy name' (*Psa.* 86:11). The Lord has promised to put his fear in our heart (*Jer.* 32:40). Let us pray over this promise: while some pray for riches, and others for children, let us pray for a heart to fear God.

To conclude this, you who have this fear planted in your souls, bless God for it: 'Ye that fear the LORD, bless the LORD' (*Psa.* 135:20). God has done more for you than if he had made you kings and queens, and caused you to ride upon the high places of the earth. He has enriched you with that jewel which he bestows only upon the elect.

Oh, stand upon Mount Gerizim, blessing. The fear of God is an immortal seed springing up into glory: 'Ye that fear the LORD praise him' (*Psa.* 22:23). Begin the work of heaven now. Be spiritual choristers: sound forth holy doxologies and triumphs. Say, as David, 'Let my mouth be filled with thy praise, and with thy honour all the day' (*Psa.* 71:8).

God has but little praise in the world. Who should thus pay that which is due to him, if not they that fear him?

7

THE GODLY SHOULD
SPEAK OF GOD

Having done with the character of the godly in general terms, I proceed next to their special characteristics: They 'spake often one to another'. When the wicked said, 'It is vain to serve God', then 'they that feared the LORD spake often one to another'. The meaning of this word, they 'spake often', is they discoursed religiously together; their tongues were divinely tuned by the Holy Spirit.

Christians, when they meet together, should use holy conference. This is not only an advice, but a charge: 'These words . . . shall be in thine heart: and thou shalt . . . talk of them when thou sittest in thine house, and when thou walkest by the way, and when thou liest down, and when thou risest up' (*Deut.* 6:6). Indeed, where there is *gratia infusa* [grace poured in], it will be *effusa* [poured out]; grace changes the language, and makes it spiritual. When the Holy Spirit came upon the apostles, they spoke 'with other tongues' (*Acts* 2:4). Grace makes Christians speak with other tongues. A good Christian not only has the law of God in his heart (*Psa.* 37:31), but in his tongue (verse 30). The body is the temple of God (*1 Cor.* 6:19). The tongue is the organ in this temple, which sounds in holy discourse; 'The tongue of the just is as choice silver' (*Prov.* 10:20). He drops silver sentences, enriching others with knowledge: 'A good man out of the good treasure of his heart bringeth forth good things' (*Matt.* 12:35). In his heart is a treasure of goodness, and this is not like a bag of money sealed, but he brings something out of the treasure within to the enriching of others. Grace is of the nature of fire, which will not be pent up; like new wine it requires a vent (*Acts* 4:20). There is a principle within that constrains to holy conference: 'The spirit within me constraineth me' (*Job* 32:18).

The *first use* of this doctrine is for *information*. It shows the genius and temper of true saints: they 'speak often one to another'; their lips drop as a honeycomb. The country to which a man belongs is known by his language. He who belongs to the Jerusalem above speaks the language of Canaan; none of God's children is dumb; their mouth is a 'wellspring of wisdom' (*Prov.* 18:4).

The *second use* is *reproof*. Here I may draw up a bill of indictment against five sorts of persons.

1. Such as are silent in matters of religion. They would be counted good, but he must have good eyes that can see it! I know not whether it be ignorance or bashfulness that sets good discourse aside. Many are as mute in religion as if their tongues did cleave to the roof of their mouth. Had they any love to God, or had they ever tasted how sweet the Lord is, their mouth would 'talk of his righteousness'

(*Psa.* 71:24). Friends, what should concern us but salvation? What are the things of this world? They are neither real or lasting (*Prov.* 23:5). Do we not see men heap up riches, and suddenly death, as God's sergeant, arrests them? What should we talk of but the things pertaining to the kingdom of God? Let this cause blushing among Christians, that their meetings are so unprofitable, because they leave God out of their discourse. Why is there no good conference? Have you so much knowledge that you need not have it increased? Have you so much faith that you need not have it strengthened? Silence in religion is a loud sin! We read of one who was possessed with a dumb devil (*Mark* 9:17). How many are spiritually possessed with a 'dumb devil'!

2. It is a rebuke to such as, when they meet together, instead of speaking of heaven, have idle, frothy discourse. They *talk* but do not *say* anything, as Plutarch[1] said of Alcibiades. Their lips do not drop as a honeycomb, but run as a spout; their speaking is just like a child's scribbling. 'They speak vanity every one with his neighbour' (*Psa.* 12:2). If Christ should ask some today, as he did the two disciples going to Emmaus, what manner of communications they have as they walk (*Luke* 24:17), they could not answer as those did, 'Concerning Jesus of Nazareth'; no, perhaps about toys, or new fashions. If idle words must be accounted for (*Matt.* 12:36), Lord, what an account will some have to give!

3. It reproves the avaricious person who, instead of speaking of heaven, talks of nothing but the world: the

---

[1] Plutarch (AD c. 46-c. 127), Greek historian, biographer, and essayist.

farmer speaks of his plough and yoke of oxen, the trades-man of his wares and drugs; but not a word of God. 'He that is of the earth speaketh of the earth' (*John* 3:31). Many are like the fish in the gospel that had money in its mouth (*Matt.* 17:27). They talk only of secular things, as if they imagined to fetch happiness out of that earth which God has cursed.

Seneca, being asked of what country he was, answered he was 'a citizen of this world'. We may know many to be citizens of this world. Their speech betrays them. *O curvae in terras animae, et coelestium inanes* (O souls bent towards the earth and empty of spiritual things).[1]

4. It reproves those who do indeed speak often to one another, but in a bad sense.

i. They speak one to another in hasty words. Their words should be like the 'waters of Shiloah that go softly' (*Isa.* 8:6), but too often they are fierce and pungent. Water, when it is hot, soon boils over; when the heart is heated with anger it soon boils over in furious speeches (*James* 3:6). Passion transports.

Many curse in their anger. The tongue is made in the fashion of a sword, and it cuts like a sword. Angry words often prejudice him that utters them. Rehoboam with one churlish word lost ten tribes. A fiery spirit is unsuitable to the Master we serve, the Prince of Peace; and to his ambassage, the 'gospel of peace'. Such whose tongues are set on fire, let them take heed that they do not one day in hell desire a drop of water to cool their tongue (*Luke* 16:24).

---

[1] *Satires* of Persius (AD 34–62), Roman poet, 2.61.

ii. They speak one to another in a bad sense who murmur and complain one to another; they do not complain of their sins, but their needs. Murmuring proceeds from unbelief: 'They believed not his word: but murmured' (*Psa.* 106:24–25). When men distrust God's promises, they murmur at his providences. This is a sin God can hardly bear: 'How long shall I bear with this evil congregation, which murmur against me?' (*Num.* 14:27). Israel's speeches were venomous, and God punished them with venomous serpents (*1 Cor.* 10:10).

iii. They speak one to another in a bad sense who give vent to filthy, scurrilous language. The heart is a cask full of wickedness, and the tongue is the tap that lets it flow out. When the face breaks out in sores and pimples, it shows the blood is corrupt. When men break forth in unsavoury speeches it shows the heart is profane. 'Evil communications corrupt good manners' (*1 Cor.* 15:33). We read that the lips of the leper were to be covered (*Lev.* 13:45). It would be a benefit if we had such magistrates as would, by their authority, cover the unclean lips of these lepers.

iv. They speak one to another in a bad sense who, instead of seasoning their words with grace, mix them with oaths. Swearers rend and tear God's name and, like mad dogs, fly in the face of heaven. 'Because of swearing the land mourneth' (*Jer.* 23:10). Some think it graceful speech to mix every sentence with an oath; as if they would go to hell genteelly. 'But', says one, 'it is my custom to swear.' Is this an excuse or an aggravation of the sin? If a malefactor should be arraigned for robbery, and he should say to the judge, 'Spare me for it is my custom to rob on the highway', the judge would say, 'You shall the rather die.' For every oath that a man swears, God puts a drop of wrath into his vial.

5. It reproves those who, instead of speaking in a holy manner one to another, speak one *of* another:

First, in *censuring*. Some make it a part of their religion to talk about and criticize others. They do not imitate their graces but reflect upon their failings. God grant that professors may wash their hands of this! Were people's hearts more humble, their tongues would be more charitable. It is the sign of a hypocrite to censure others and commend himself.

Secondly, they speak one of another in *slandering*: 'Thou slanderest thine own mother's son' (*Psa.* 50:20). Slandering is when we speak to the prejudice of another, and speak that which is not true. Worth is blasted by slander. Holiness itself is no shield from this sin. The lamb's innocency will not preserve it from the wolf. Job calls slandering 'the scourge of the tongue' (*Job* 5:21). You may smite a man yet never touch him. A slanderer wounds another's fame, and no physician can heal these wounds. The eye and the name are two tender things. God takes it ill at our hands to calumniate others, especially to slander those who help to keep up the credit of religion: 'Were ye not afraid to speak against my servant Moses?' (*Num.* 12:8). What, my servant, who has wrought so many miracles, whom I have spoken with in the mount face to face! Were you not afraid to speak against him? The Greek word for *slanderer* signifies *devil*

(*1 Tim.* 3:11). This is the devil's proper sin, he is 'the accuser of the brethren' (*Rev.* 12:10). He does not commit adultery, but he bears false witness. The slanderer may be indicted for clipping; he clips his neighbour's credit to make it weigh lighter. This our nature is prone to; but remember, it is just as much a sin in God's reckoning to break the Ninth Commandment as the Eighth.

The *third use* is *exhortation*. Put this great duty into practice. Imitate these holy ones in the text, they 'spake often one to another'. Jerome thinks they spoke something in defence of the providence of God; they vindicated God in his dealings, and exhorted one another not to be discouraged at the virulent speeches of the wicked, but still to hold on a course of piety. Thus, Christians, when you meet, give one another's souls a visit, drop your knowledge, impart your experiences to each other (*Psa.* 66:16). Samson having found honey did not only eat of it himself, but carried it to his father and mother (*Judg.* 14:9). Have you tasted the honey of the Word? Let others have a taste with you.

He who has been in a perfumer's shop does not only himself partake of those sweet smells, but some of the perfume sticks to his clothes, so that those who come near him partake of those perfumes: so having ourselves perceived the sweet savour of Christ's ointments, we should let others partake with us, and by our heavenly discourse, diffuse the perfume of religion to them. Let your words be seasoned with salt (*Col.* 4:6). Let grace be the salt which seasons your words and makes them savoury. Christians should take all occasions of good discourse when they walk together, and sit at table together. This makes their eating and drinking to be 'to the glory of God' (*1 Cor.* 10:31). What makes it a communion of saints but good conversation?

But some may say they are barren of matter, and know not what to speak of. No, have you walked so often through the field of Scripture, yet gathered no ears of corn? Have not you matter enough in the Word to furnish you with something to say? Let me suggest a few things to you. When you meet, speak one to another of the *promises*. No honey so sweet as that which drops from a promise. The promises are the support of faith, the springs of joy, the saints' royal charter. Are you citizens of heaven, and yet do not speak of your charter?

Speak of the *preciousness of Christ*: he is beauty and love; he has laid down his blood as the price of your redemption. Have you a friend who has redeemed you, and never speak of him?

Speak one to another of *sin*, what a deadly evil it is, how it has infected your virgin-nature, and turned it into a lesser hell.

Speak of the beauty of *holiness*, which is the souls embroidery, filling it with such oriental splendour as makes God and angels fall in love with it. The graces are (as Damascen[1] says) the sacred 'characters and impressions of the divine nature'.

Speak one to another of your *souls*: enquire whether they are in health.

---

[1] John of Damascus (c. AD 675–c. 749), Greek theologian.

Speak about *death and eternity:* can you belong to heaven and not speak of your country?

Speak one to another of the *times,* wherein God is the greatest sufferer: let your hearts bleed for his dishonours. Thus, you see, here is matter enough for holy conference. Why then do you not set good discourse on foot? I believe that one main reason for the decay of the power of godliness is a lack of Christian conference. People when they meet talk of impertinencies, but God and heaven are left out of their discourse. That I may persuade you in your conversations to put in a word about your souls, let me offer these few things for your consideration.

1. *It was the practice of the saints of old.* Elijah and Elisha went on in good discourse till the chariot of heaven came to part them (2 *Kings* 2:11). David's tongue was tuned to the language of Canaan: 'My tongue shall talk of thy righteousness' (*Psa.* 71:24). The primitive Christians, into whatever company they came, spoke of a glorious kingdom they expected, so that some thought they were ambitious of worldly honour. Justin Martyr said in their defence that the kingdom they looked for was not of this world but a kingdom with Christ in heaven. Jerome says that some of the Roman ladies spent much of their time in communing together, and would not let him alone, but continually asked him questions about their souls.

2. *We are bidden to redeem the time (Eph.* 5:16). The poets painted time with wings because it flies so fast. Time lost must be redeemed, and is there any better way to redeem time, than to improve it in trading for heaven, and speaking of God and our souls?

3. *Jesus Christ has left us a pattern.* His words were perfumed with holiness, 'All bare him witness, and wondered at the gracious words which proceeded out of his mouth' (*Luke* 4:22). Christ had grace poured into his lips (*Psa.* 45:2). In all companies he set good discourse on foot. When he sat on Jacob's well he falls into an heavenly discourse with the woman of Samaria about the water of life (*John* 4:14). And so when Levi made him a feast (*Luke* 5:29), he feasts him again with heavenly discourse. And no sooner was Christ risen from the grave but he 'was speaking of the things pertaining to the kingdom of God' (*Acts* 1:3). The more spiritual we are in our speeches, the more we resemble Christ. Should not the members be like the Head? Christ will not be our Saviour unless we make him our pattern.

4. *Good discourse would prevent sinful discourse.* Much sin passes in ordinary talk, as gravel and mud pass along with water. How many are guilty of tongue-sins! Good discourse would prevent evil, as labour prevents idleness. If we accustomed our tongues to the heavenly dialect, the devil would not have so much power over us.

5. *We may guess at men's hearts by their common discourse. Verba sunt speculum mentis* – Words are the looking glass of the mind (Bernard). As you may judge of a face by the mirror, whether it be fair or foul; so by the words we may judge of the heart. A lascivious tongue shows a lustful heart, an earthly tongue a covetous heart; a gracious tongue, a gracious heart. The Ephraimites were known by their pronunciation, saying 'sibboleth' for 'shibboleth' (*Judg.* 12:6). So by the

manner of our speech it may be known to whom we belong. The tongue is the index of the heart. If you broach a cask, that which is within will come out. By that which comes out of the mouth, you may guess what is within, in the heart: 'Of the abundance of the heart his mouth speaketh' (*Luke* 6:45).

6. *Good discourse is beneficial:* 'How forcible are right words!' (*Job* 6:25). A word spoken in season may make such a powerful impression upon another's heart that it will do him good all his life. One single coal is apt to die, but many coals put together keep in the heat. Christians by their heavenly talk may 'blow up' one another's grace into a flame.

Monica, Augustine's mother, hearing others discourse of heaven, was greatly affected and cried out, 'What do I do here? Why is my soul held any longer with this earthen fetter of my flesh?'

When the daughters of Jerusalem had conversed a while with the spouse, and had heard her describe Christ's admirable beauty, their affections began to be enflamed, and they would seek him with her. 'Whither is thy beloved gone, O thou fairest among women . . . that we may seek him with thee?' (*Song of Sol.* 6:1).

A Christian by divine discourse may enlighten another when he is ignorant, warm him when he is frozen, comfort him when he is sad, confirm him when he is wavering. Latimer was much strengthened by discourse with Thomas Bilney in prison, and hearing his confession of faith. A good life adorns religion, a good tongue propagates it. When the apostle would have us edify one another, what better way could he prescribe than this, to have such holy speeches proceed out of our mouths as might 'minister grace unto the hearers' (*Eph.* 4:29)?

7. *We must be accountable to God for our speeches.* Words are judged light, but they weigh heavy in God's balance. By our words we shall be either saved or damned: 'For by thy words thou shalt be justified, and by thy words thou shalt be condemned' (*Matt.* 12:37). If our words have been seasoned with grace, then the acquitting sentence is likely to go on our side.

8. *Good discourse is a Christian's honour.* The tongue is called our glory (*Psa.* 30:12), because it is the instrument of glorifying God. When our tongues are out of tune in murmuring, then they are not our glory; but when the organs sound in holy discourse, then our tongues are our glory.

9. *Good discourse will be a means to bring Christ into our company.* While the two disciples were conferring about the death and sufferings of Christ, Jesus Christ himself came among them: 'While they communed together . . . Jesus himself drew near, and went with them' (*Luke* 24:15). When bad discourse is set on foot, Satan draws near and makes one of the company; but when good discourse is promoted, Jesus Christ draws near.

Let all that has been said excite good conference. Certainly, there is no better way than this to increase our stock of grace. Others by spending grow poor; but the more we spend ourselves in holy discourse, the richer we grow in grace, as the widow's oil, by pouring out, increased (2 *Kings* 4).

QUESTION: How may good conference be arrived at?

ANSWER 1: If you wish to discourse of religion, get your minds well furnished with knowledge. Hereby, you will have a treasure to fetch from. 'I am', says Elihu, 'full of matter' (*Job* 32:18). Some are backward to speak of good things for lack of matter. The empty vessel cannot run. If you would have your tongues run fluently in religion, they must be fed with a spring of knowledge: 'Let the word of Christ dwell in you richly' (*Col.* 3:16). In one of the miracles that Christ wrought, he first caused the water-pots to be filled with water, and then said, 'Draw out now' (*John* 2:8). So we must first have our heads filled with knowledge, and then we shall be able to draw out to others in good discourse.

ANSWER 2: If you would discourse readily in the things of God, make religion your delight. What men delight in, they will be speaking of. The sensualist speaks of his sports; the worldling of his rich purchase. Delight makes the tongue as the pen of a ready writer. The spouse, being delighted and enamoured with Christ's beauty, could not conceal herself; she makes an elegant and passionate oration in the commendation of Christ. 'My beloved is white and ruddy, the chiefest among ten thousand' (*Song of Sol.* 5:10).

ANSWER 3: Pray that God will both gift and grace you for Christian conference: 'O Lord open thou my lips' (*Psa.* 51:15). Satan has locked up men's lips. Pray that God will open them. Perhaps you pray that you may believe in Christ, but do you pray that you may confess him, and not be ashamed to speak of him before others?

'I will speak of thy testimonies also before kings, and will not be ashamed' (*Psa.* 119:46). To end this, let me briefly insert two cautions:

CAUTION 1: I do not deny that it is lawful to confer of worldly business sometimes; communication requires conference. But with this proviso, that we should show more delight and earnestness in speaking of spiritual things than earthly, remembering that the soul is far more valuable than the world.

CAUTION 2: When persons speak of religion, let it not be for any sinister, unworthy end, nor for ostentation, but for edification; and then, having your aim right, speak of the things of God with life and affection, that others may perceive you feel those truths of which you speak.

8

THE GODLY SHOULD
MEDITATE ON GOD'S NAME

The second special characteristic of the godly in the text is, they thought upon God's name. These saints, when they were together, *spoke of God;* when they were alone they *thought of God:* they 'thought upon his name'.

QUESTION: What is meant by God's name?

ANSWER 1: By the name of God is meant his *essence;* God's name is put for God himself.

ANSWER 2: By the name of God is meant his glorious *attributes*, which are, as it were, the several letters of his name.

ANSWER 3: By the name of God is meant his *worship and ordinances* where his name is called upon: 'Go ye now unto my place which was in Shiloh, where I set my name at the first' (*Jer.* 7:12). That is, where I first set up my public worship.

Now this name of God, the saints in the text did contemplate, they thought upon his name. Thoughts are the first-born of the soul, the conceptions of the mind, the immediate fruit and issue of a rational being. 'Thoughts are the representations of things in the imagination' (Moller)[1]. These devout souls in the text were chiefly busying their thoughts about God and heaven.

It is the inseparable sign of a godly man to employ his chief thoughts about God: 'The thoughts of the righteous are right' (*Prov.* 12:5); that is, they are set upon the right object. It is natural to think. Thoughts fly out of the mind as sparks out of a furnace. The Hebrew word for a thought signifies the boughs of a tree, because thoughts shoot out from our minds as branches do from a tree. It is, I say, natural to think, but it is not natural to think of God; this is proper to a saint. His thoughts are sublime and seraphical, they fly to heaven.

The mind is a mint-house where thoughts are minted. David minted golden cogitations: 'I am still with thee' (*Psa.* 139:18), that is (as learned Ainsworth[2] expounds it), by divine contemplation. Thoughts are travellers in the soul. David's thoughts kept heaven-road: 'I am continually with thee' (*Psa.* 73:23). As the mariners needle turns to the North Pole so a saint's thoughts are still pointing towards God.

QUESTION: Whence is it that the saints' thoughts mount up to God?

ANSWER 1: There will be this thinking on God from those *intrinsic perfections* which are in him. The loveliness of the object attracts the thoughts. God is the supreme good. There is nothing but God worth thinking

[1] Henri Moller (1528–89), Professor at the Wittenberg Academy and friend of Melanchthon.

[2] Henry Ainsworth (1571–1622), Congregational Minister and Bible commentator.

upon. 'Thou art my portion, O Lord' (*Psa.* 119:57). Will not a man's thoughts run upon his portion? A gracious soul has found pleasure in thinking on God (*Psa.* 63:5–6). He has had those transfigurations on the mount, those comings in of the Spirit, those enterings of God's love, those prelibations and foretastes of glory, so that he cannot keep his thoughts off from God. To hinder him from thinking on God is to bar him of all his pleasure.

Answer 2: There will be thinking on God from the *powerful operations of the Holy Spirit*. We cannot of ourselves think a good thought (2 *Cor.* 3:5), but the Spirit elevates and fixes the heart on God: 'The Spirit lifted me up' (*Ezek.* 3:14). When you see the iron move upward, you know there has been some magnet drawing it. So when the thoughts move upwards towards God, the Spirit has, as a divine magnet, drawn them.

First Use: *Reproof.*

Out of the quiver of this text I may draw several arrows of reproof:

1. It reproves *such as do not think upon God's name.*

It is the brand-mark of a reprobate: 'God is not in all his thoughts' (*Psa.* 10:4). He endeavours to expunge and blot God out of his mind. Though he draws his breath from God, yet he does not think of him: his thoughts shoot into the earth (*Phil.* 3:19). Had not sinners by their fall lost their head-piece, they would reason thus with themselves: Certainly God is best worth thinking on. Is there any excellency in the world? Then what is there in God that made it? He gives the star its beauty, the flower its fragrance, food its pleasantness; and if there be such deliciousness in the creature, what is in God? He must needs be better than all. O my soul, shall I admire the drip and not the ocean? Shall I think of the workmanship, and not of him that made it? This is the fruit of original sin: it has warped the soul, and taken it off from the right object.

2. It reproves *such as indeed think of God, but who do not have right thoughts of him.* As the Lord said to Eliphaz 'Ye have not spoken of me the thing that is right' (*Job* 42:7); so some think of God, but they do not think of him the thing that is right.

i. They have low unworthy thoughts of God, they fancy God to be like themselves (*Psa.* 50:21). Men think God is as short-sighted as they, and that he cannot see them through the thick canopy of the clouds: but he that makes a watch knows all the wheels and pins in it, and the spring which causes the motion. God who is the inspector of the heart (*Acts* 1:24; 15:8) sees all the intrigues and private cabals in the thoughts (*Job* 42:2; *Amos* 4:13). God knows the true motion of a false heart: 'I know, and am a witness, saith the LORD' (*Jer.* 29:23).

ii. Men have injurious thoughts of God: *First,* they deem his ways unequal: 'Is not my way equal?' (*Ezek.* 18:25). Some call God's providence to the bar of reason, and judge his proceedings eccentric; but God 'lays righteousness to the plummet' (*Isa.* 28:17). His ways are secret, but always just. God is most in his way when we think he is out of his way. *Secondly,* they think his ways are not profitable: 'What profit is it that we have kept his ordinance?'

(*Mal.* 3:14). We cannot show our earnings. These are not right thoughts of God. Men think him to be a hard master; but God will be in no man's debt, he gives double pay: 'Neither do ye kindle a fire on my altar for nought' (*Mal.* 1:10).

3. It reproves *such as, instead of thinking on God, have their minds wholly taken up with vain thoughts.* Vain thoughts are the froth of the brain: 'How long shall thy vain thoughts lodge within thee?' (*Jer.* 4:14). I do not deny that vain thoughts may sometimes come into the best hearts, but they have a care to turn them out before night, that they do not lodge. This denominates a wicked man. His thoughts dwell upon vanity; and well may his thoughts be said to be vain, because they do not turn to any profit: 'Vanity, and things wherein there is no profit' (*Jer.* 16:19). They are vain thoughts which are about foolish things, and run all into straw. They are vain thoughts which do not better the heart, nor will give one drop of comfort at death: 'In that very day his thoughts perish' (*Psa.* 146:4). Vain thoughts are pernicious; they taint the heart and leave an ill tincture behind.

4. It reproves *such as have, not only vain thoughts, but vile thoughts.*

Firstly, proud thoughts: while they view themselves in the mirror of self-love, they begin to take up venerable thoughts of themselves, and so pride fumes up into their head and makes them giddy (*Acts* 5:36). Secondly, impure thoughts. They think how to gratify their lusts, they 'make provision', or as the word signifies, become 'caterers' for the flesh (*Rom.* 13:14).

Sin begins in the thoughts; first men devise sin, then act it (*Mic.* 2:1–2). For instance, if one seeks preferment, he thinks to himself by what ladder he may climb to honour. He will cringe and comply, and lay aside conscience, and this is the way to rise. If a man would grow rich, he sets his thoughts to work how to compass an estate; he will circumvent, and pull down his soul to build up an estate. Would he wreak his malice on another? He frames a plan in his thoughts to take away his life: as Jezebel (that painted harlot) when she would ruin Naboth, presently feigns a sham-plot and subtly thinks of a way how to dispatch him: 'Proclaim a fast and set Naboth on high among the people, and set two men, Sons of Belial to witness against him, saying, thou didst blaspheme God and the King, and carry him out and stone him' (*1 Kings* 21:9–10).

Oh, the mischief of thoughts! A man may deny God in his thoughts: 'The fool hath said in his heart there is no God' (*Psa.* 14:1). He may commit adultery in his thoughts: 'Whosoever looks on a woman to lust after her hath committed adultery with her in his heart' (*Matt.* 5:28). A man may murder another in his thoughts: 'Whosoever hateth his brother is a murderer' (*1 John* 3:15). O how much contemplative wickedness is in the world! Tremble at sinful thoughts. We startle at gross sin, but we are not troubled so much for sinful thoughts. Know firstly, that sin may be committed in the thoughts, though it never blossom into outward act: 'The thought of foolishness is sin' (*Prov.* 24:9). See this illustrated in two things: Envy—the Jews envied Christ the fame of his miracles: 'Pilate knew that for envy they had delivered him' (*Matt.* 27:18). Here was sin committed in the thoughts: the Jews sinned by envying Christ, though they had never crucified him. Discontentment—'Cain was wroth and his countenance fell' (*Gen.* 4:5). He maligned his brother, and his thoughts boiled up to discontentment. Here was sin committed in the thoughts. Cain sinned by being discontented, even if he had never murdered his brother.

Know, secondly, that God will punish sinful thoughts. We say thoughts are free; so they are in man's court; but God will punish for thoughts: it was set upon Herod's score that he thought to destroy Christ under a pretence of worshipping him (*Matt.* 2:8).

Let us be humbled for the sins of our thoughts. 'If thou hast thought evil, lay thy hand upon thy mouth' (*Prov.* 30:32); that is, humble and abase yourself before the Lord. The best alive need to be humbled for their thoughts:

First, for the instability of their thoughts. How do the thoughts dance up and down in prayer. Like quicksilver, they will not fix. It is hard to tie two good thoughts together. Secondly, for the impiety of their thoughts. In the fairest fruit may be a worm, and in the best heart evil thoughts may arise. Did men's hearts stand where their faces do, they would blush to look one upon another. Let us, I say, be deeply humbled for our thoughts. Let us look up to Christ that he would stand between us and God's justice, and that he would intercede for us, that the thoughts of our hearts may be forgiven us.

SECOND USE: *Exhortation.*

Let us think of God's Name; let us lock up ourselves with God every day; let our thoughts get wings and, with the birds of paradise, fly up towards heaven. Christians, look upon that day to be lost, in which you have not conversed with God in your thoughts; think of God in your closet, in your shop; trade above the moon. 'Isaac went out to meditate in the field' (*Gen.* 24:63). He walked in heaven by holy utterances. Our minds should be steeped in holy thoughts.

It is not enough to have a few transient thoughts of God by the by, but there must be a fixing of our minds on God, till our hearts are warmed in love to him, and we can say, like those in Luke 24:32, 'Did not our heart burn within us?'

But what should the matter of our holy meditations be?

1. Think of God's *immense being*. Adore his illustrious attributes, which are the beams by which the divine nature shines forth. Think of God's omniscience. He particularly and critically assesses all our actions, and notes them down in his daybook. Think of God's holiness, which is the most sparkling jewel of his crown (*Exod.* 15:11).

Think of God's mercy: this makes all his other attributes sweet. Holiness without mercy, and justice without mercy, would be terrible. Think of God's veracity: 'Abundant in . . . truth' (*Exod.* 34:6); that is, God will be so far from coming short of his word that he does more than he has said. He shoots beyond the promise, never short of it.

2. Think of the works of God: 'I will meditate also of all thy work' (*Psa.* 77:12). God's works are bound up in three great volumes, *Creation, Redemption, Providence*: here is sweet matter for our thoughts to expatiate upon.

To enforce the exhortation, let me propose some *arguments and inducements to be frequent in the thoughts of God*.

1. The reason why God has given us a thinking faculty is that we may think on his Name. When our thoughts run out in things not pertinent (like water running past the mill) we should think with ourselves thus: Did God give us a talent to misemploy? Did he give us thoughts that we should think of everything but him? Were these arrows given us to shoot beside the mark?

2. If we do not accustom ourselves to good thoughts, we cannot be good Christians. Thinking seriously on heavenly things makes them stay in our minds, causes delight in them, and makes them nourish us. Musing on holy objects is like digesting food, which turns it into blood and spirits; so that, without holy thoughts, there is no religion. Can a man be religious and scarcely ever think of it?

3. We are deeply obliged to think on God. For, first, God is our Maker: 'It is he that hath made us, and not we ourselves' (*Psa.* 100:3). Our bodies are God's curious needlework (*Psa* 139:15). And as God has wrought the cabinet, so he has put a jewel in it, the precious soul. Has God made us, and shall not we think of him? Secondly, God has sweetened our lives with various mercies. The

city of Syracuse in Sicily was so curiously situated that the sun was never out of sight. God has so placed us by his providence that the sunshine of mercy is never out of sight. We are miraculously attended with mercy; mercy feeds us with the finest of the wheat, the bread of life; mercy guards us with a guard of angels; it makes the rock pour forth rivers of oil: and shall not the stream lead us to the fountain? Shall not we think of the God of our mercies? This were high ingratitude.

4. To have frequent and devout thoughts of God witnesses sincerity. No truer touchstone of sanctity exists than the spirituality of the thoughts. What a man is, that his thoughts are: 'For as he thinketh in his heart, so is he' (*Prov.* 23:7). Thoughts are freer from hypocrisy than words. One may speak well for applause, or to stand right in the opinion of others; but when we are alone and think of God's Name, and admire his excellencies, this shows the heart to be right. Thoughts are freer from hypocrisy than an unblamable life. A man may in his outward behaviour be fair, yet have a covetous, revengeful mind. The acts of sin may be conceived when the heart sits brooding upon sin; but to have the thoughts spiritualized and set upon God is a truer symptom of sincerity, than a life free from vice. Christians, what do your thoughts run upon? Where do they make their most frequent visits? Can you say, Lord, our hearts are still mounting up to heaven, our thoughts are lodged in paradise; though we do not see thy face, yet we think on thy Name? This is a good evidence of sincerity. We judge men by their actions; God judges them by their thoughts.

5. Thinking much on God would cure the love of the world. Great things seem little to him that stands high. To such as stand upon the top of the Alps, the great cities of Italy seem like little villages. For those who are mounted high in the contemplation of Christ and glory, how do the things of the world disappear, and even shrink into nothing! A soul elevated by faith above the visible planets, has the moon under his feet. A true saint intermeddles with secular affairs more out of necessity than choice. St Paul's thoughts are sublime, he lived in the altitudes, and how he scorned the world! 'The world is crucified unto me' (*Gal.* 6:14).

6. Thinking on God would be expulsive of sin. From whence is impiety but from thoughtlessness? If only men carefully considered God's holiness and justice, would they dare sin at the rate they do? That which kept Joseph in check was the thought of a sin-revenging God. When the delights of sin tickle, let the thoughts of God come into men's minds, that he is both Spectator and Judge, and that after the golden crowns and women's hair come the lions' teeth (*Rev.* 9:8). This would put them into a cold sweat, and be as the angel's drawn sword (*Num.* 22:31). It would scare them from sin.

7. Thinking on God is an admirable means to increase our love to God. As it was with David's meditations on mortality – 'As I was musing the fire burned' (*Psa.* 39:3) – so it is with our musing on the Deity: while we are thinking on God, our hearts will kindle in love to him. The reason our affections are so chilled and cold in religion is that we do not warm them with the thoughts of

God. Hold a magnifying glass to the sun, and the glass burns that which is near to it. So when our thoughts are lifted up to Christ, the Sun of righteousness, our affections are set on fire. No sooner had the spouse been thinking upon her Saviour's beauty but she fell *sick of love* (*Song of Sol.* 5:8). O saints, do but let your thoughts dwell upon the love of Christ, who passed by angels and thought of you; who was wounded that, out of his wounds, the balm of Gilead might come to heal you; who leaped into the sea of his Father's wrath, to save you from drowning. Think of this unparalleled love which sets the angels wondering, and see if it will not affect your hearts and cause tears to flow forth.

8. Thinking on God will by degrees transform us into his image. As Jacob's flock looking on the rods that had white streaks conceived and *brought forth like them* (*Gen.* 30:39), so by contemplating God's holiness, we are in some measure changed into his likeness: 'Beholding as in a glass the glory of the Lord, we are changed into the same image' (2 *Cor.* 3:18). The contemplative sight of God was transforming: they had some print of God's holiness upon them; as Moses when he had been on the mount with God, his face shone (*Exod.* 34:35). What is godliness but God-likeness? And who are so like him as those that think on his name?

9. Thinking on God is sweet. It ushers in a secret delight to the soul: 'My meditation of him shall be sweet' (*Psa.* 104:34). He whose head gets above the clouds has his thoughts lifted high, has God in his eye, is full of divine raptures, and cries out as Peter in the transfiguration,

'Lord, it is good to be here.' Holy thoughts are the dove we send out of the ark of our souls, and they bring an olive branch of peace. Some complain that they have no joy in their lives; and truly, no wonder, when they are such strangers to heavenly contemplation. Would you have God give you comfort, and never think of him? Indeed Israel had manna dropped into their tents, and they never thought of it; but God will not drop down this manna of heavenly joy on that soul which seldom or never thinks of him. Would you have your spirits cheerful? Let your thoughts be heavenly. The higher the lark flies, the sweeter it sings; the higher a soul ascends in the thoughts of God, the sweeter joy it has.

10. Thoughts of God will turn to the best account. Thoughts spent on the world are often in vain. Some spend thoughts about laying up a portion for a child; and perhaps either it dies, or lives to be a cross. Others beat their brains how to rise at court; and when royal favour has shone upon them, all of a sudden an eclipse comes about, the king's smile is turned into a frown, and then their thoughts are frustrated.

How oft do men build castles in the air? But the thoughts of God will turn to a good account, they augment sanctification, and bring satisfaction: 'My soul shall be satisfied as with marrow and fatness . . . when I remember thee upon my bed, and meditate on thee', etc. (*Psa.* 63:5–6). The thoughts we have of God in the time of health, will be a comfort to us in the time of sickness.

11. God thinks of us, and shall not we think of him? 'The Lord thinketh upon me' (*Psa.* 40:17). God thinks on us

every morning; his mercies are 'new every morning' (*Lam.* 3:23). He gives us night-mercies, he rocks us every night asleep: 'So he giveth his beloved sleep' (*Psa.* 127:2); and if we wake, he gives 'songs in the night' (*Job* 35:10). If God is thinking of us day and night, shall not we think of his Name? How can we forget a friend who is ever mindful of us? 'I know the thoughts that I think toward you, saith the LORD, thoughts of peace' (*Jer.* 29:11). Though God be out of our sight, we are not out of his thoughts.

12. God will one day reckon with us for our thoughts. He will say, 'I gave you a cogitative faculty. What have you done with it?' If God asks a covetous man, 'What have your sentiments been? Which way have your thoughts run?', He will answer, 'To heap up riches.' If God asks princes and emperors, 'How have you employed your thoughts?', they will say, 'How by our sceptre to beat down the power of godliness.' What a dreadful account will these persons have to give at last! Not only men's actions but their thoughts will accuse them (*Rom.* 2:15).

13. Our thoughts of God shall not be lost. God accepts the thought for the deed. David had a good thought come into his mind to build God a house, and God took it as kindly as if he had done it: 'Forasmuch as it was in thy heart to build an house for my name, thou didst well in that it was in thy heart' (2 *Chron.* 6:8). When Christians have thoughts of promoting God's glory, they would do such good acts if it were in their power, build hospitals, distribute justice, cut off offenders from the city of God, the Lord looks upon it as if they had done it; so that our thoughts of God are not lost.

Let us think of God in a right manner. A good medicine may be spoiled in the making. So may a good duty be spoiled in the doing. Thoughts may be good for the matter of them, yet may be faulty in the manner. I shall show you, first, how thoughts of God may fail in their manner; then, the right manner of thinking upon God.

1. *How thoughts of God may fail in their manner.*

First, a man may think of God, yet not intend his glory. Jehu had good thoughts come into his mind, to destroy the Baal-worshippers, but his intent was to advance himself into the throne. Bad aims spoil good actions. *Secondly,* a man may have good thoughts but they are forced. When one bleeds under God's afflicting hand, he may think of God, yet have no love to him: 'When he slew them, then . . . they remembered that God was their rock, and the high God their Redeemer: nevertheless they did flatter him with their mouth' (*Psa.* 78:34–36). These were good thoughts, but it was to pay God a compliment in order to get rid of the affliction. *Thirdly,* a man may have thoughts of God out of a design to stop the mouth of conscience. Conscience lashes the profane sinner: 'What! Are you so wicked as never to think of God, who indulges you with so many favours?' Hereupon he may have a few good thoughts; but they are irksome to him: this is not from a principle of conscience, but to quiet conscience. *Fourthly,* a man may think of God with horror: he thinks of God's sovereignty, and dreads the thoughts of God. You see one may think of God, yet these thoughts may become sinful.

2. *The right manner of thinking upon God.*

First, our thoughts of God must be serious. Feathers swim on the suface but gold sinks into the water. Feathery spirits have some floating thoughts; but good hearts sink deep in the thoughts of a Deity. *Secondly,* our thoughts of God must be spiritual. Take heed of framing any gross conceits of God in your minds, representing him by the likeness of the creature: 'Ye saw no similitude' (*Deut.* 4:15). Conceive of God in Christ: we cannot see him any other way, as we cannot see the sun in the circle, but in the beams: the Godhead dwells in Christ's human nature (*Col.* 2:9). Think of God as a Spirit full of immense glory, propitious to us through a Mediator. *Thirdly,* our thoughts of God must be delightful. With what delight does a child think of his father! A gracious soul counts them the sweetest hours which are spent with God. *Fourthly,* our thoughts of God must be operative and efficacious, leaving our hearts in a better tune. The thoughts of God's faithfulness must make us confide in him; the thoughts of God's holiness must make us conform to him. This is the right thinking on God when it is influential, leaving us in a more heavenly frame.

Third Use: *Direction.*

The text shows us how to have our thoughts frequently fixed upon God.

1. *Begin the day with holy thoughts:* 'When I awake, I am still with thee' (*Psa.* 139:18). God should have the first buddings of our thoughts. In the law, the Lord would have the first fruits offered him. Give God your virgin-

thoughts in the morning. What the vessel is first seasoned with, it keeps the relish of a long time after. The mind seasoned with good thoughts in the morning will keep the heart in a better state all the day after.

2. *If you would think of God, take heed of hindrances.*

i. *Turn away your eyes from beholding vanity (Psa. 119:37)*. Vain objects poison the imagination, lascivious pictures and wanton talk leave bad impressions there.

ii. As far as you are able, *call your thoughts off from the world*. If worldly thoughts come crowding into our mind, good thoughts will be lost in the crowd.

iii. *Get a love for God and his ways.* One cannot but think of that which he loves: 'Can a maid forget her ornaments?' (*Jer.* 2:32). When she has not her jewel on her ear, she will have it in her thoughts. A person deeply in love cannot keep his thoughts off from the object he loves. The reason we think on God no more, is because we love him no more. Let there be but one spark of love to God and it will fly upward in heavenly thoughts and prayers. By nature we have quicksilver hearts which cannot be made to fix on God, but by love.

iv. If you would think often on God, *get an interest in him*: 'This God is our God' (*Psa.* 48:14). We think most upon that which is our own. If a man ride by handsome houses and gardens, he casts his eyes slightly upon them; but let him have a house of his own and his thoughts dwell in it. Why do men think no more of God, but because God and they are strangers? Let a man's interest in God be cleared and he will not be able to keep his thoughts off from God.

PART TWO

THE GOOD EFFECTS
OF GODLINESS

And they shall be mine, saith the LORD *of hosts, in that day when I make up my jewels; and I will spare them, as a man spareth his own son that serveth him. Then shall ye return, and discern between the righteous and the wicked, between him that serveth God, and him that serveth him not*
(Mal. 3:17–18).

9

GOD REGARDS THE PIETY
OF HIS PEOPLE

The first of the good effects of the saints' piety is that God regarded it: 'The LORD hearkened, and heard.'

These blessed ones in the text were speaking and thinking of God, and he did not turn away his ear from them, as if he had not minded them; but he *hearkened and heard*; which expression denotes both diligence and delight.

1. *It notes the diligent heed God gave to these saints, he 'hearkened'*. Here was attention of ear, and intentness of mind. Hearkening is the gesture of one that listens to what another says.

2. *God's hearkening shows the delight he took in the holy dialogues of these saints*. He was pleased with them; they were to him as sweet melody.

God takes special notice of the good which he sees in his people. The children of God may perhaps think that God does not regard them: 'I cry unto thee, and thou dost not hear me' (*Job* 30:20). The church complains that God shuts out her prayer (*Lam.* 3:8), but though God is sometimes silent, he is not deaf: he takes notice of all the good services of his people: 'The LORD hearkened and heard.'

Whence is it that God takes such notice of his people's services?

First, *not from any merit in them*, but the impulsive cause is his free grace. The best duties of the righteous could not endure God's scales of justice, but God will display the trophies of his mercy. Free grace accepts what justice might condemn.

Secondly, God's taking notice of the good in his people is *through Christ*: 'He hath made us accepted in the beloved' (*Eph.* 1:6). Or, as Chrysostom renders it, he has made us 'favourites'. Through a red glass every thing appears of a red colour; through Christ's blood, both our persons and duties appear ruddy and beautiful in God's eyes.

Thirdly, God takes notice of the services of his people, *because they flow from the principle of grace*. God regards the voice of faith: 'O my dove . . . let me hear thy voice; for sweet is thy voice' (*Song of Sol.* 2:14). The services of the wicked are harsh and sour, but the godly give God the first-ripe cluster (*Mic.* 7:1), which grows from the sweet and pleasant root of grace.

FIRST USE: *Information.*

1. If God hearkens and hears, I infer hence *God's omniscience*. How could he, being in heaven, hear what the saints speak and think, were he not omniscient? Through the bright mirror of his own essence he has a full

idea of all things. He knows the intrigues of states, the stratagems of his enemies (*Exod.* 14:24). Future contingencies fall within his cognizance. God's knowledge is primary: he is the original, pattern, and prototype of all knowledge. God's knowledge is instantaneous. He knows all at once: our knowledge is successive, we know one thing after another, and argue from the effect to the cause; but all things are in God's view *uno intuitu*, in one entire prospect. God's knowledge is infallible and not subject to mistake. Such is the infinity of his knowledge, that the apostle cries out in admiration, 'O the depth of the riches both of the wisdom and knowledge of God!' (*Rom.* 11:33). The world is to God as a beehive of glass, where you see the working of the bees and the framing of their combs. All things are unveiled to the eye of Jehovah.

2. See God's *goodness,* who often passes by the failings of his people (*Num.* 23:21), and takes notice of the good in them. 'Sarah obeyed Abraham, calling him Lord' (*1 Pet.* 3:6). The Holy Ghost passes by her unbelief and laughing at the promise, and takes notice of her reverence to her husband; she called him Lord. 'Ye have heard of the patience of Job' (*James* 5:11). We have heard of his impatience, cursing his birth day, but the Lord does not upbraid him with that but observes the good that was in him: 'Ye have heard of the patience of Job'. The painter who drew Alexander's picture, drew him with his finger upon his scar; so God puts a finger of mercy upon the scars of his children. He sees their faith, and turns a blind eye to their failings.

3. See God's *differing dealings towards the godly and the wicked*. If the godly think of his name, he hearkens and hears; but if the wicked meddle with religious duties, he turns away his ear. 'Unto Cain and to his offering he had not respect' (*Gen.* 4:5). Suppose a man had a sweet breath, yet if he had the plague, nobody would come near him; so, though a sinner may give God many a sweet, elegant expression in prayer, yet, having the plague in his heart, God will not receive any offering from him. If God shuts men's prayers out of heaven, it is a sad prognostic that he will shut their persons out of heaven.

4. See *the privilege of the godly:* they have God's ear, 'the LORD hearkened and heard'; 'His ears are open unto their cry' (*Psa.* 34:15): It would be counted a great happiness to have the king's ear; but what is it to have God's ear? Believers have the Spirit of God breathing in them, and God cannot but hear the voice of his own Spirit.

5. See *what an encouragement is here to be conversant in the duties of God's worship:* he takes notice of the services of his people; he hearkens to them as to sweet music. Who would not come with their humble addresses to God, when he is so pleased with them (*Prov.* 15:8)?

OBJECTION 1: *But I deserve nothing.*

ANSWER: God does not bestow his favours according to our desert, but according to his promise.

OBJECTION 2: *But I have prayed a long time and have no answer.*

ANSWER: God may *hear* prayer when he does not *answer*. He may lend us his ear when he does not show us his face. The text says, 'the LORD hearkened and heard.' It is not said he gave an answer, but he 'hearkened'. It becomes suitors to wait. Faith stays upon God, patience stays for God: 'As the eyes of servants look unto the hand of their masters . . . so our eyes wait upon the LORD our God, until that he have mercy upon us' (*Psa.* 123:2).

6. See *the difference between God and men*: God takes notice of the good in his people; the wicked pass by the good in the godly, and take notice only of their failings. If they can spy any impropriety or blemish in them, they upbraid them with it; like those children who reproached Elisha for his baldness, but took no notice of the prophet's miracles (2 *Kings* 2:23). Erasmus speaks of one who observed all the deficient verses in Homer but passed over the good.

7. From the words, 'the LORD hearkened and heard', take note of *the folly of idolaters:* they worship a God who can neither hearken nor hear. The Cretans pictured Jupiter without ears. Idol gods have ears, but hear not (*Psa.* 115:6). A lifeless God is good enough for a lifeless worship.

SECOND USE: *Exhortation.*

1. Let the people of God *stand and wonder:*

i. *At God's condescension*, that he who is so high in the praises and acclamations of the angels should stoop so low as to listen to the lispings of his children. 'The LORD hearkened and heard': alas, God has no need of our services; he is infinitely blessed in reflecting upon the splendour of his own infinite being: we cannot add the least cubit to his essential glory: 'If thou be righteous, what givest thou him? or what receiveth he of thine hand?' (*Job* 35:7). Yet such is his sweet condescension that he does as it were stoop below himself, and take notice of his peoples poor offerings.

ii. *At God's love*, that he should regard those services of his people, which are so mixed with corruption: 'Our righteousnesses are as filthy rags' (*Isa.* 64:6). The sacrifice of thanksgiving, which was the highest, had some leaven joined with it (*Lev.* 7:13). Our best duties have some leaven of imperfection in them; yet such is God's love, that he has a liking to them, and accepts them: 'I have eaten my honeycomb with my honey' (*Song of Sol.* 5:1). Honey is sweet, but the honeycomb is viscous and bitter, and can hardly be eaten; yet such was Christ's love to his spouse, that he ate of her honeycomb, her services mixed with imperfection, and was pleased to take delight in them. Oh, the love of God, that he should have respect to our offerings that are interlaced with sin! Our best duties are sweet wine coming out of a sour cask.

2. If God hearkens to us when we speak, *let us hearken to him when he speaks*. In the Word preached God speaks to us. He is said now to speak to us from heaven (*Heb.* 12:25), that is, by the preaching of the Word, as a king speaks by his ambassador. Does God hearken to us, and shall not we hearken to him? Be not like the deaf adder which stops her ear. This the Lord complains of: 'God speaketh once, yea twice; yet man perceiveth it not' (*Job* 33:14). If God's Word does not prevail with us, our prayers will not prevail with him.

10

GOD RECORDS THE PIETY OF HIS PEOPLE

The second good effect of the saints' piety was that God recorded it. 'A book of remembrance was written before him'; the word in the original for 'book of remembrance' signifies 'a book of memorials' or 'monuments'. The words immediately foregoing recite God's hearkening and hearing; but lest any should say, though God does at the present hear the holy speeches and thoughts of his children, yet may they not in time slip out of his mind? Therefore these words are added, 'a book of remembrance was written before him.' The Lord did not only hear the good speeches of the saints, but recorded them, and wrote them down: 'A book of remembrance was written.'

This is spoken after the manner of men; not that God has any book of records by him. He does not need to write down anything for the help of his memory. He is not subject to forgetfulness. Things done a thousand years ago are as fresh to him as if they were done but yesterday: 'A thousand years in thy sight are but as yesterday when it is past' (*Psa.* 90:4).

This 'book of remembrance', therefore, is a borrowed form of speech, taken from kings, who have their chronicles wherein they note memorable things (Grotius).[1] King Ahasuerus had his book of records, wherein were written the worthy deeds of Mordecai (*Esther* 6:1–2). So God bears in mind all the good speeches and pious actions of his children. God's particular and critical assessment is a *book of records*, where nothing can be lost or torn out.

DOCTRINE: *God eternally remembers all the good designs and pious endeavours of his people:* 'God is not unrighteous to forget your work and labour of love, which ye have shewed towards his name (*Heb.* 6:10). There are eight things which God writes down in his book of remembrance.

1. The Lord writes down the *names* of his saints: 'whose names are in the book of life' (*Phil.* 4:3). This book has no *errata* (*Rev.* 3:5).

2. The Lord writes down the *good speeches* of his people. When Christians speak together of the mysteries of heaven (which is like music in concert), God is much taken with it. When their tongues are going, God's pen is going in heaven. 'They that feared the LORD spake often one to another, and a book of remembrance was written.'

3. The Lord writes down the *tears* of his people. Tears drop down to the earth, but they reach heaven: God has his bottle and his book: 'Put thou my tears into thy bottle: are they not in thy book?' (*Psa.* 56:8). Tears drop from the saints as water from the roses: they are fragrant to God, and he puts them in his bottle. And besides this,

---

[1] Hugo Grotius (1583–1645), Dutch jurist and statesman.

he has his book of remembrance, where he sets them down: 'Are they not in thy book?' Especially God writes down such tears as are shed for the sins of the times. One was 'clothed with linen, with a writer's inkhorn by his side' (*Ezek.* 9:2). This was to write down the tears of the mourners, and to 'set a mark upon the foreheads of the men that sigh and cry for all the abominations that be done in the midst' of the city (verse 4).

4. God writes down the *thoughts* of his people. We can write down men's words, but we cannot write down their thoughts. It would perplex the angels to write men's thoughts. But be assured, never a holy thought comes into our mind but God writes it down. So in the text a book of remembrance was written for them that thought upon his name. Two things are silent, yet have a voice: tears (*Psa.* 6:8), and thoughts (*Isa.* 66:18).

5. God writes down the *desires* of his people: 'All my desire is before thee' (*Psa.* 38:9); that is, 'It is set down in thy book.' Desire is the spiritual appetite, or the soul's panting and breathing after God (*Psa.* 84:2). In this life we do rather desire God than enjoy him. Can we say that we take our souls *e corporis pharetra*, out of the quiver of our bodies and shoot them into heaven? Do our affections sally forth towards Christ? Do we desire him superlatively and incessantly? Every such desire is put down in God's register book: 'All my desire is before thee.'

6. The Lord writes down the *prayers* of his people (*Jon.* 2:7). Prayer, though it be not vocal, only mental, is recorded, 'Hannah spake in her heart' (*1 Sam.* 1:13). That prayer did God write down and answer. God was better

to her than her prayer; she prayed for a son and God gave her a prophet. At times the heart is so full of grief that it can only groan in prayer; yet a groan is sometimes the best part of a prayer, and God writes it down: 'Lord . . . my groaning is not hid from thee' (*Psa.* 38:9). If we cannot speak with elegance in prayer, if it be only lisping and chattering, God puts it in his book of remembrance: 'Like a crane or a swallow, so did I chatter' (*Isa.* 38:14); yet that prayer was heard and registered, 'I have heard thy prayer, I have seen thy tears' (verse 5).

7. God writes down the *alms* of his people. Works of mercy must be done out of love to God. As Mary out of love brought her ointments and sweet spices and anointed Christ's dead body, so out of pure love we must bring our ointments of charity to anoint the saints, which are Christ's living body. Such alms are not lost. With such sacrifices God is well pleased (*Heb.* 13:16). And that we should see how well the Lord is pleased with them, he writes them down thus: '*item,* so much lent to the Lord.' 'Thine alms are come up for a memorial before God' (*Acts* 10:4).

8. God has a book of remembrance for the *sufferings* of his people. The saints' purgatory is in this life. But there are two things which may bear up their spirits.

First, every groan of theirs goes to God's heart: 'I have also heard the groaning of the children of Israel' (*Exod.* 6:5). In music when one string is touched, all the rest sound. When the saints are stricken God's heart reverberates.

Secondly, God has a book of records to write down his people's injuries. The wicked make wounds in the backs of the righteous, and then pour in vinegar. God writes down their cruelty: 'I remember that which Amalek did to Israel' (*1 Sam.* 15:2). Amalek was Esau's grandchild (*Gen.* 36:12), a bitter enemy of Israel. The Amalekites showed their spite to Israel in two ways. First, they lay in ambush; and as Israel passed by, fell upon their rear, and cut off the feeble in their army (*1 Sam.* 15:2). Secondly, they openly gave battle to them and would have hindered them from going into Canaan (*Exod.* 17:8). Now God took notice of Israel's sufferings by Amalek: 'I remember what Amalek did to Israel, and I have my book of remembrance; I write it down.' 'Now go and smite Amalek' (*1 Sam.* 15:3).

FIRST USE of the doctrine: *Information.*

1. It shows us that *it is not in vain to serve God.* The wicked who know not God think him a hard master, and say, like those Job speaks of, 'What profit should we have, if we pray unto him?' (*Job* 21:15). But the text shows us that God records all the services of his people, 'a book of remembrance was written before him.' God's writing in a book is:

i. *An honour to the saints.* The Romans wrote the names of their senators in a book, and in token of honour they were called *Patres conscripti,* the chosen fathers of the people. So God's book of remembrance shows his high esteem of his people and their services. He writes them down.

ii. *A mark of the special favour God bears to his people.* He registers them and their services, with an intent to crown them. Tamerlane[1] wrote down all the memorable deeds of his soldiers, whom he afterwards preferred to places of dignity. God's service is most desirable; let us make Joshua's choice: 'As for me and my house, we will serve the LORD' (*Josh.* 24:15).

If we should desert God's service, where shall we go? When Christ asked his disciples, Will you also go away? Peter said, 'Lord, to whom shall we go?' (*John* 6:68); as if to say, 'If we leave thee, we do not know where to get help for ourselves.' Let us adhere to God; he has his book of memorials to record our allegiance. We may be losers *for* him, but we shall not be losers *by* him.

2. See from this that, as God registers the good works of his people, so he has a book of remembrance *to write down the sins of the wicked*: 'Go, write it before them in a table, and note it in a book, that it may be for the time to come for ever and ever, that this is a rebellious people . . . that will not hear the law of the LORD' (*Isa.* 30:8–9). Men's sins are written in the book of conscience, and the book of God's omnisciency. They think because God does not speak to them by his loud judgments, therefore God does not know their sins. But though God does not speak, he writes: 'The sin of Judah is written with a pen of iron, and with the point of a diamond' (*Jer.* 17:1). God scores down every act of oppression, bribery, uncleanness: 'They consider not in their heart that I remember all their wickedness' (*Hos.* 7:2). King Belshazzar was carousing and drinking wine in bowls, and praising his gods of gold and

---

[1] Tamerlane or Tamburlaine: (c. 1336-1405), Tartar conqueror.

silver; but while he was sinning, God was writing: 'In the same hour came forth fingers of a man's hand, and wrote . . . upon the plaster of the wall of the king's palace, and the king saw the part of the hand that wrote. Then the king's countenance was changed' (*Dan.* 5:5–6). We read of God's book: 'The books were opened' (*Rev.* 20:12); and we also read of his bag: 'My transgression is sealed up in a bag' (*Job* 14:17). This seems to allude to law courts where indictments against malefactors are sealed up in a bag, and produced at the assizes.

When God shall open his black book in which men's names are written, and his bag in which their sins are written, then their hearts will tremble and their knees smite one against another. Every lie a sinner tells, every oath he swears, every drunken bout, God writes it down in his book of remembrance; and woe to him if the book is not crossed out with the blood of Christ!

3. See *the mercifulness of God to his children,* who blots their sins out of his book of remembrance, and writes their good deeds in his book of remembrance: 'I, even I, am he that blotteth out thy transgressions' (*Isa.* 43:25). This is a metaphor borrowed from the case of a creditor who takes his pen and blots out the debt owing to him; so says God, I will 'blot out thy transgressions'. Or as the Hebrew has it, 'I *am blotting* them out.'

God in forgiving sin passeth an act of oblivion or amnesty (forgetting): 'I will remember their sin no more' (*Jer.* 31:34). God will not upbraid his people with their former offences. We never read that when Peter repented

Christ upbraided him for his denial of his Lord. Oh, the heavenly indulgence and kindness of God to his people! He remembers everything but their sins. He writes down their good thoughts and speeches in a merciful book of remembrance; but their sins are as if they had never been; they are carried into the land of oblivion.

SECOND USE: *Exhortation.*

If God records our services, then *let us record his mercies;* let us have our book of remembrance. A Christian should keep two books always beside him; one to write his sins in, that he may be humble; the other to write his mercies in, that he may be thankful. David had his book of remembrance: 'He appointed certain of the Levites . . . to record, and to thank and praise the LORD God of Israel' (*1 Chron.* 16:4). We should keep a book to record God's mercies – though I think it will be hard to get a book big enough to hold them. At such and such a time we were in straitened circumstances, and God supplied us; at another time under sadness of spirit, and God dropped in the oil of gladness; at another near death, and God miraculously restored us. If God be mindful of what we do for him, shall not we be mindful of what he does for us? God's mercies, like jewels, are too good to be lost: get a book of remembrance.

THIRD USE: *Comfort.*

It is comfort to the godly:

1. *In the case of friends forgetting them.* Joseph did Pharaoh's butler a kindness, 'Yet did not the chief butler

remember Joseph, but forgat him' (*Gen.* 40:23). It is only too usual to remember injuries, and forget friends; but God has a book of remembrance where he writes down all his old friends. Near relations may sometimes be forgetful. The tender mother may forget her infant: 'Can a woman forget her sucking child? . . . yea, they may forget, yet will I not forget thee' (*Isa* 49:15). A mother may sooner be unnatural than God forgetful. Christ our high priest has the names of the saints written upon his breastplate, and all their good deeds written in his book of memorials. Let this be a Bezar stone[1] to revive the hearts of God's people; though friends may blot you out of their mind, yet God will not blot you out of his book.

2. This is consolation to the godly, the Lord keeps a book of remembrance for this end, *that he may at the last day make a public and solemn mention of all the good which his saints have done*. God will open his book of records and say, 'I was an hungred, and ye gave me meat; thirsty, and, ye gave me drink', etc. (*Matt.* 25:35–36).

God will make known all the memorable and pious actions of his people before men and angels: he will say, Here are those who have prayed and wept for sin; here are those who have been advocates for my truth; here are those who have laid to heart my dishonours, and have mourned for what they could not reform. These are my renowned ones, my *Hephzibahs* in whom my soul delights (*Isa.* 62:4).

---

[1] Bezar or Bezoar stones were concretions from the kidneys of an Arabian wild goat, believed to be a potent charm against the plague and poison.

What a glorious thing will this be, to have God express the high praise of his saints! When Alexander saw the sepulchre of Achilles, he cried out 'O happy Achilles, who had Homer to set forth thy praise!' What an honour will it be to have the names and worthy deeds of the saints mentioned, and God himself to be the herald to proclaim their praises (2 *Cor.* 4:5)!

11

GOD REWARDS THE PIETY
OF HIS PEOPLE

The third good effect of the saints' piety was that God rewarded it: 'And they shall be mine, saith the LORD of hosts, in that day when I make up my jewels' (*Mal.* 3:17). The reward is threefold.

1. *God's owning them:* 'They shall be mine, saith the LORD of hosts.'
2. *God's honouring them:* 'In that day when I make up my jewels.'
3. *God's sparing them:* 'I will spare them, as a man spareth his own son that serveth him.'

Note first, the Person speaking, 'the LORD of hosts'. This is too great a word to be passed by in silence. God is often in Scripture styled, *Dominus exercituum*,[1] 'the LORD of hosts' (*Psa.* 46:11; *Isa.* 1:24); that is, he is the Supreme General, and Commander of all armies and forces, and gives victory to whom he will.

QUESTION: Why is this name, 'the LORD of hosts', given to God?

---

[1] This is the rendering used in the Latin Vulgate Bible of Jerome.

ANSWER: Not because God needs any hosts to protect himself, or suppress his enemies. Earthly princes have armies to defend their persons from danger, but God needs none to help him: he can fight without an army. God puts strength into all armies. Other captains may give their soldiers armour; they cannot give them strength; but God does: 'Thou hast girded me with strength unto the battle' (*Psa.* 18:39). Why then is God said to have hosts and armies if he needs them not?

Firstly, it is to set forth his sovereign power, and grandeur; all armies and regiments are under his command.

Secondly, it is to show us that though God can effect all things by himself; yet in his wisdom he often uses the agency of the creature to bring to pass his will and purpose.

QUESTION: What are these hosts or armies of which God is the sovereign Lord?

ANSWER 1: God has an army in heaven, *angels and archangels:* 'I saw the LORD sitting on his throne, and all the host of heaven standing by him' (*1 Kings* 22:19). By the host of heaven is meant the angels; they, being spirits, are a powerful army: 'Ye his angels, which excel in strength' (*Psa.* 103:20). We read of one angel who destroyed in one night 'an hundred fourscore and five thousand' (*2 Kings* 19:35). If one angel destroyed such a vast army, what can a legion of angels do? A legion consisted of six thousand, six hundred and sixty six, says Hesychius:[1] how many of

---

[1] Probably Hesychius of Alexandria, lexicographer, late-4th and early-5th century AD.

these legions go to make up the heavenly host! (*Dan.* 7:10).

The *stars* are God's army too (*Deut.* 4:19). These were set in battalions and fought against God's enemies: 'The stars in their courses fought against Sisera' (*Judg.* 5:20). That is, the stars charged like an army, raising storms and tempests by their influences, and so destroying the whole army of Sisera.

ANSWER 2: God has armies upon earth, both *rational* and *irrational*. The *rational* are hosts of men. These are under God's command and conduct. They do not stir without his warrant. The Lord has the managing of all martial affairs. Not a stroke is struck, but God orders it. Not a bullet flies, but God directs it. As for the *irrational*, God can raise an army of flies, as he did against King Pharaoh (*Exod.* 8:24); an army of worms, as he did against King Herod (*Acts* 12:23). Oh, what a Lord is here, who has so many hosts under his pay and conduct!

FIRST USE of the doctrine: *Exhortation.*

1. *Let us dread this Lord of hosts.* We fear men who are in power, and is not that God to be adored and feared who acts at his pleasure? He does 'according to his will in the army of heaven, and among the inhabitants of the earth' (*Dan.* 4:35). His power is as large as his will: 'What his soul desireth, even that he doeth' (*Job* 23:13). The *Ephori* had power over the king of Sparta; the tribunes over the Roman consuls; much more has God a sovereign power over all. 'He poureth contempt upon princes' (*Job* 12:21). He threw the proud angels to hell. God can with

a word unpin the wheels and break the axle-tree of the creation. God's power is a glorious power (*Col.* 1:11). And in this it appears glorious: it is never spent or wasted. Men, while they exercise their strength, weaken it. But 'the LORD, the Creator of the ends of the earth, fainteth not, neither is weary' (*Isa.* 40:28). Though God 'spends his arrows' upon his enemies (*Deut.* 32:23), yet he spends not his strength.

Oh, then tremble before this Lord of hosts! Remember, O hard-hearted sinner, how many ways God can be revenged on you. He can raise an army of diseases against you in your body. He can set the humours of the body[1] one against another, he can make the heat dry up the moisture, or the moisture drown the heat. He can arm every creature against you, the dog, the boar, the elephant. He can arm conscience against you, as he did against Spira[2] making him a terror to himself. Oh, dread this Lord of hosts.

2. If God is the Lord of hosts, *let us take heed of hardening our hearts against God*. It was the saying of Pompey[3] that with one stamp of his foot he could raise all Italy up in arms. God can with a word raise all the militia of heaven and earth against us, and shall we dare affront him? 'Who hath hardened himself against him, and hath prospered?' (*Job* 9:4). Such as live in the open breach of

---

[1] In the old physiology the humours were fluids thought to permeate the body and determine health and temperament.

[2] Francis Spira (d. 1548), Italian convert to Protestantism who returned to Roman Catholicism and died in despair.

[3] Pompey (106–48 BC), distinguished military and political leader of the late Roman republic.

God's commandments harden their hearts against God; they raise a war against heaven: 'He strengtheneth himself against the Almighty' (*Job* 15:25). Like warriors who muster up all the forces they can to fight with their antagonists, so the sinner hardens and strengthens himself against Jehovah: 'He runneth upon him, even on his neck, upon the thick bosses of his bucklers' (verse 26). Bucklers anciently had one great boss in the middle with a sharp spike in it to wound the adversary. The grossly wicked sinner encounters the God of heaven and runs upon the thick bosses of his fury, which will wound mortally. The wicked do as Caligula,[1] who challenged Jupiter to a duel; but who ever hardened himself against God and prospered? Will men go to measure arms with God? 'Hast thou an arm like God?' (*Job* 40:9).

God is almighty, and therefore can hurt his enemies; and he is invisible, therefore they cannot hurt him. Who can fight with a spirit? God will be too hard for his enemies in the long run: 'God shall wound the head of his enemies, and the hairy scalp of such an one as goeth on still in his trespasses' (*Psa.* 68:21). Julian[2] hardened his heart against God, but what did he get at last? Did he prosper? Being wounded in battle he threw up his blood into the air, and said to Christ, *Vicisti Galilæe*: 'O Galilean, thou hast overcome; I acknowledge thy power whose name and truth I have opposed.'

How easily can God chastise rebels! 'In the morning watch the LORD looked unto the host of the Egyptians

[1] Caligula, third Roman Emperor, assassinated AD 41.
[2] Julian the Apostate (AD 331-363), Roman emperor who tried to restore paganism.

through the pillar of fire and of the cloud, and troubled the host of the Egyptians' (*Exod.* 14:24). It need cost God no more to destroy his proudest adversaries than a look, a cast of the eye. It is better to lie prostrate at God's feet, and to meet him with tears in our eyes rather than weapons in our hands. We overcome God, not by resistance, but by repentance.

3. If God is the Lord of hosts, *let us be so wise as to engage him on our side.* 'The LORD of hosts is with us' (*Psa.* 46:11). Great is the privilege of having the Lord of hosts for us!

i. If the Lord of hosts is on our side, *he can discover the subtle plots of enemies.* Thus he detected the counsel of Ahithophel (2 *Sam.* 17:14). And did not the Lord discover the Popish conspirators, both in the Powder Treason[1] (that Catholic villainy) and of late, when they would have subverted religion and laws and, like Italian butchers, turned England into an Aceldama, or field of blood?[2] If it had not been the Lord who was on our side, now may *England* say, when men rose up against us, then they had swallowed us up quick (*Psa.* 124:1–3).

ii. If the Lord of hosts is on our side, *he can bridle his enemies* and lay such a restraint upon their spirits that they shall not do the mischief they intend: 'It is in the power of my hand to do you hurt (said Laban to Jacob): but the God of your father spake unto me . . . saying, Take thou heed that thou speak not to Jacob either good or bad' (*Gen.* 31:29). Laban had power to do hurt, but no

---

[1] The Gunpowder Plot of 1605.
[2] The 'Popish Plot' of 1678, fabricated by Titus Oates.

heart. When Balak called upon Balaam to curse Israel, God so dispirited Balaam that he could not discharge his thunderbolt: 'How shall I curse, whom God hath not cursed?' (*Num.* 23:8). He had a good mind to curse, but God held him back.

iii. If the Lord of hosts is for us, *he can help us, though means fail, and things seem to be given up for lost*. When Gideon's army was small, and rendered despicable, then God crowned them with victory (*Judg.* 7:2, 22). When the arm of flesh shrinks, then is the time for the arm of omnipotency to be put forth: 'The LORD . . . shall repent himself for his servants, when he seeth that their power is gone, and there is none shut up or left' (*Deut.* 32:36). The less seen of man, the more of God.

iv. If the Lord is on our side, *he can save us in that very way in which we think he will destroy us*. Would not any have thought that the great fish's belly should have been Jonah's grave? But God made a fish a ship in which he sailed safe to shore. Paul got to land by the breaking of the ship (*Acts* 27:44). God can make the adverse party do his work; he can cause divisions among the enemies, and turn their own weapons against themselves: 'I will set the Egyptians against the Egyptians' (*Isa.* 19:22; *Judg.* 7:22).

v. If the Lord of hosts is on our side, *he can make the church's affliction a means of her augmentation*: 'The more they afflicted them, the more they multiplied' (*Exod.* 1:12). The church of God is like that plant of which Gregory Nazianzen[1] speaks which lives by dying, and grows by cutting. Persecution propagates the church:

---

[1] Gregory Nazianzen (AD 330–389), Cappadocian church father.

the scattering of the apostles up and down was like scattering seed: it did tend much to the spreading of the gospel (*Acts* 8:1, 4).

vi. If the Lord of hosts is on our side, *he can alter the scene and turn the balance of affairs when he pleases:* 'He changeth the times and the seasons' (*Dan.* 2:21). God can remove mountains which lie in the way, or leap over them. His power is uncontrollable; he can bring harmony out of discord. He who brought Isaac out of a dead womb, and the Messiah out of a virgin's womb, what can he not do? The Lord of hosts can in an instant alter the face of things. There are no impossibilities with God. If *means* fail, he can *create*. It is therefore high prudence to get this Lord of hosts on our side. 'If God be for us, who can be against us?' (*Rom.* 8:31).

And if we would engage God to be on our side:

First, let us be earnest suitors to him, exercise eyes of faith, and knees of prayer (*Jer.* 14:9). And in prayer let us use Joshua's argument, 'What wilt thou do unto thy great name?' (*Josh.* 7:9). Lord, if the cause of religion lose ground, how will thy name suffer! Popish enemies never prevail, but they blaspheme.

Secondly, let us put away iniquity out of our tabernacles (*Job* 11:14). Sin is not worth keeping. Who would keep a plague sore? Let us discard and abjure our sins (*Jer.* 7:3); and then the Lord of hosts will be on our side and, as a pledge of his favourable presence, he will entail the gospel, that crowning blessing, upon us and our posterity.

So much for the Person speaking, 'the Lord of hosts'.

12

GOD REWARDS HIS PEOPLE BY OWNING THEM

I come now to the reward itself, the first part of which is God's owning them, 'They shall be mine.'

Expositors here vary. I take the sense of it to be, 'They shall be mine in covenant'; 'I . . . entered into a covenant with thee . . . and thou becamest mine' (*Ezek.* 16:8; *Isa* 43:1). This is no small favour, to be in covenant with God. Therefore, when God told Abraham that he would enter into covenant with him, Abraham fell on his face (*Gen.* 17:3), as being amazed that the great God should bestow such a signal favour upon him. God never entered into covenant with the angels when they fell, but he proclaims himself God in covenant with believers, 'They shall be mine.' This covenant enriched with free grace is a better covenant than that which was made with Adam in innocence, for:

1. *The least failing would have made the first covenant null and void*, but many failings do not invalidate the covenant of grace. I grant the least sin makes a trespass upon the covenant, but it does not cancel it. Every failing in the conjugal relation does not break the marriage bond.

2. If the first covenant was violated, the sinner had no remedy; all doors of hope were shut. But the new covenant allows of a remedy. It provides a Surety, 'Jesus the mediator of the new covenant' (*Heb.* 12:24).

FIRST USE: *Information.*

See the amazing goodness of God to his people, to enter into covenant with them and say, 'You are mine.' 'He hath made with me an everlasting covenant, ordered in all things and sure' (2 *Sam.* 23:5). The first covenant stood upon the ticklish foundation of works. Adam had no sooner a stock of original righteousness to trade with than he broke the covenant. But this covenant of grace is confirmed with God's decree, and rests upon two mighty pillars, the *oath* of God, and the *blood* of God. That you may see how great a privilege it is to be owned by the Lord federally, consider:

1. If we are in covenant with God and he saith to us 'You are mine', then *all that is in God is ours*. A person falling on hard times and then marrying a king has a share in all the crown revenues. God having entered into a near relation with us and saying, 'You are mine', we have a share in his rich revenues. The Lord says to every believer, as the King of Israel said to the King of Syria, 'I am thine, and all that I have' (*1 Kings* 20:4); my wisdom shall be yours to teach you, my holiness shall be yours to sanctify you, my mercy shall be yours to save you. What richer dowry than Deity? God is a whole ocean of blessedness. If there is enough in him to fill the angels, then sure he has enough to fill us.

2. If God says to us, 'You are mine', then *he will have a tender care of us*. 'He careth for you' (*1 Pet.* 5:7). God, to show his tender solicitude towards Israel, bore them 'on eagles' wings' (*Exod.* 19:4). The eagle carries her young ones upon her wing to defend them; the arrow must first shoot through the old eagle, before it can touch her young ones. A mother's care is seen in leading a child so that it may not fall. Such is God's care: 'I taught Ephraim also to go, taking them by their arms' (*Hos.* 11:3). We may argue from the lesser to the greater, that if God takes care of the meanest insects and animals that creep upon the earth, much more will he take care of his covenant saints. He is still consulting and projecting for their good; if they wander out of the way, he guides them; if they stumble, he holds them by the hand; if they fall, he raises them; if they become dull, he quickens them by his Spirit; if they are perverse, he draws them with cords of love; if they are sad, he comforts them with his promises.

3. If God says to us, 'You are mine', then *he will entirely love us:* 'I have loved thee with an everlasting love' (*Jer.* 31:3). The Lord may give a man riches and not love him; his prosperity may be as Israel's quails, sauced with God's wrath (*Num.* 11:32–33). But when God says, 'You are mine', he cannot but love; every one loves his own. If God has any love better than another, his covenant people shall have it; he will extract the essence of his love for them; he loves them as he loves Christ (*John* 17:23).

4. If God says to us, 'You are mine', then *he will not suffer us to be in need*. Believers are not only of God's

family, but of Christ's body; and will the Head let the body starve? 'Verily thou shalt be fed' (*Psa.* 37:3). God has not promised dainties; he will not satisfy his people's lusts, but he will supply their needs. If the bill of fare should be restricted, what they lack in cheer they shall have in blessing: 'He shall bless thy bread, and thy water' (*Exod.* 23:25). God will rather work a miracle than that any of his children shall famish. The raven is so unnatural that she will hardly feed her young, yet she became a caterer and brought food to the prophet Elijah.

5. If God says to us, 'You are mine', then *we have great immunities:*

i. *We are freed from the revenging wrath of God.* We are not free from God's anger as a Father, but as a Judge. God will not pour his vindictive justice upon us. Christ has drunk the red wine of God's wrath upon the cross, that believers may not taste a drop of it.

ii. *We are freed from the predominant reign of sin:* 'Sin shall not have dominion', or as the word is, it shall not '*lord it* over you' (*Rom.* 6:14). Though believers are not freed from the in-being of sin, nor from the combat with it, yet they are freed from its imperious command. As it is said of those beasts in Daniel, 'They had their dominion taken away: yet their lives were prolonged for a season' (*Dan.* 7:12), so sin lives in the regenerate, but its dominion is taken away. And to be thus freed from the jurisdiction, power, and tyranny of sin is no small blessing. A wicked man is at the command of sin, as the ass is at the command of the driver. The curse of Ham is upon him, 'a servant of servants shall he be' (*Gen.* 9:25). He is a slave to his lusts, and a slave to Satan. Oh, what a privilege it is to have one's neck out of the devil's yoke!

iii. *We are freed from the accusations of conscience.* The worm of conscience is part of the torment of hell. But, God being *our* God, we are freed from the clamours of this hellish fury. Conscience sprinkled with Christ's blood speaks peace; a good conscience, like the bee, gives honey; it is like the golden pot which had manna in it (2 *Cor.* 1:12).

6. If God says to us, 'You are mine', *we shall be his forever:* 'This God is our God for ever and ever' (*Psa.* 48:14). You cannot say you have health, and you shall have it forever; you have a child, and you shall have it forever; but if God is your God, you shall have him forever. The covenant of grace is a royal charter, and this is the happiness of it, it is made for eternity. Justification is never rescinded. The interest between God and his people shall never be broken off. How false therefore is the opinion of falling from grace! Shall any whom God makes his own by federal union fall finally? Indeed if salvation has no better pillar to rest upon than man's will (as the Arminians hold) no wonder if there is falling away; but a Christian's stability in grace is built upon a surer basis, namely, God's 'everlasting (or *inviolable*) covenant' (*Isa.* 55:3). Once in Christ and ever in Christ. A star may sooner fall out of its place than a true believer be plucked away from God.

7. If God says to us, 'You are mine', *he will take us up to himself at death.* Death breaks the union between the body and the soul, but perfects the union between God

and the soul. This is the emphasis of heaven's glory, to be with God. What is the joy of the blessed but to have a clear, transparent sight of God, and to be in the sweet and soft embraces of his love forever? This has made the saints desire death, as the bride her wedding day (*Phil.* 1:23). 'Lead me, Lord, to that glory', said a holy man, 'a glimpse whereof I have seen as in a glass darkly.'

SECOND USE: *Comfort.*

Let this be for the consolation of the saints. There is a covenant union between God and them, God is theirs and they are his: 'They shall be mine, saith the LORD.' Here is a standing cordial for the godly. God looks upon them as having a propriety in them, 'They shall be *mine*.' This is comfort:

i. *In respect of Satan's accusations*. He accuses the saints first to God, then to themselves; but if God says, 'You are mine', this answers all Satan's bills of indictment. Christ will show the debt book crossed in his blood. It was a saying of Bucer,[1] 'I am Christ's, and the devil has nothing to do with me.'

ii. *In respect of poverty*. Believers are married to the king of heaven, and all that is in God is theirs. A philosopher comforted himself with this, that though he had no music or vine trees, yet he had the household gods with him. So we, though we have not the vine or fig tree, yet if God be ours and we are his, this creates joy in the most impoverished condition. And that which may raise the comfort of the godly higher, and cause a jubilation of spirit, is that

[1] Martin Bucer (1491–1551), Strasbourg Reformer.

shortly God will own his people before all the world, and say, 'These are mine.' At present the elect are not known: 'It doth not yet appear what we shall be' (*1 John* 3:2). The saints are like kings in disguise; but how will their hearts leap for joy when God shall pronounce that word, 'These are mine; the lot of free grace is fallen upon them; these shall lie forever in the bosom of my love!'

THIRD USE: *Exhortation.*

To all who are yet strangers to God: labour to get into covenant with him that he may say, 'You are mine.' Why does God woo and beseech you by his ambassadors if he is not willing to be in covenant?

QUESTION: What shall a poor forlorn creature do to get into covenant with God?

ANSWER 1: If you would be in covenant with God, *break off the covenant with sin* (*1 Sam.* 7:3). What king will be in league with him who holds correspondence with his enemy?

ANSWER 2: *Labour for faith.*

i. Faith in *the mercy of God:* 'I am merciful, saith the LORD, and I will not keep anger for ever' (*Jer.* 3:12). As the sea covers great rocks as well as little sands, so God's mercy covers great sins. Manasseh, a bloody sinner, was held forth as a pattern of mercy. Some of the Jews who had a hand in crucifying the Christ yet had their sins forgiven.

ii. Faith in *the merit of Christ*. Christ's blood is not only a sacrifice to appease God, but a propitiation to ingratiate us into God's favour, and make him look upon us with a smiling aspect (*1 John* 2:2).

13

GOD REWARDS HIS PEOPLE BY HONOURING THEM

The second part of the saints' reward is God's honouring them: 'In that day when I make up my jewels'. Here are three propositions:

1. God greatly honours his people.
2. God's people are his jewels.
3. There is a day when God will make up his jewels.

1. *God greatly honours his people.* He speaks of them here with honour: 'In that day when I make up my jewels'. 'Since thou wast precious in my sight, thou hast been honourable' (*Isa.* 43:4). Honour attends holiness. That the Lord highly honours those who fear him is evident by four demonstrations.

i. *In that he prefers them before others.* He chooses them, and passes by the rest: 'Was not Jacob Esau's brother? saith the LORD: yet I loved Jacob, and I hated Esau' (*Mal.* 1:2–3).

ii. *In that God gives them frequent visits.* It is counted an honour for a subject to have his prince visit him. Our communion is with the Father and his Son Jesus (*1 John*

1:3). The Rabbis say that Moses had one hundred and fifty conferences with God and died with a kiss from God's mouth. What greater honour for a person than to have God keep him company (*Exod.* 33:11)?

iii. *In that God makes them rich heirs,* 'joint-heirs with Christ' (*Rom.* 8:17). For a man to adopt another and make him heir to his estate is no small honour done to him. The youngest believer is an heir, yea, and an heir of the crown (*1 Pet.* 5:4). This crown he has *in promisso*, in the promise (*Rev.* 2:10), and *in primitiis*, in the first fruits (*Rom.* 8:23).

iv. *In that God sends his angels to be their servants.* Such as are God's servants have angels to be theirs: 'Are they not all ministering spirits sent forth to minister for them who shall be heirs of salvation?' (*Heb.* 1:14).

FIRST USE: Who would not be fearers of God? This makes God have an honourable esteem of them. 'All men', says Chrysostom, 'are ambitious of honour'; but the true honour comes from God (*John* 5:44).

SECOND USE: If God so honours his people, let them honour him: 'Where is mine honour?' (*Mal.* 1:6). Let the saints be God-exalters, let them lift up his name in the world, and make his praise glorious (*Psa.* 66:2). But I only glance at this.

2. *God's people are his jewels:* 'In that day when I make up my jewels'. Jewels are precious things; the Hebrew word for *jewels* signifies a *treasure.* A treasure is made up of costly things: gold, and pearls, and rubies: such a precious treasure are the saints to God.

QUESTION: In what sense are the godly jewels?

ANSWER 1: They are jewels for their *sparkling quality*. Their holiness shines and sparkles in God's eyes: 'Thou hast ravished my heart with one of thine eyes' (*Song of Sol.* 4:9), that is, graces.

ANSWER 2: The godly are jewels for their *scarcity*. Pearls are not common; so the godly are scarce and rare. There are but few of these to be found. There are many false professors (as there are bastard diamonds) but few Israelites indeed. 'Few are chosen' (*Matt.* 20:16). Among the millions in Rome, there were but few senators; among the swarms of people in the world, but few believers.

ANSWER 3: The godly are jewels for their *price*. Queen Cleopatra had two jewels that contained half the price of a kingdom. Thus the saints are jewels for their value. God esteems them at a high rate; he parted with his best jewel for them. Christ's precious blood was shed to ransom these jewels.

ANSWER 4: The saints are jewels for their *adorning quality*. Jewels adorn those that wear them. The saints are jewels that adorn the world. Their piety mixed with prudence honours the gospel. Hypocrites eclipse religion and make it evilly spoken of. The saints as jewels render it illustrious by their sanctity.

FIRST USE: *Information.*

1. *See the worth of the godly:* they are jewels; 'a royal diadem in the hand of thy God' (*Isa.* 62:3). That is, they are eminent above others, as a crown hung with jewels is

a sign of the highest state and honour. The saints are God's glory (*Isa.* 46:13), as if God's glory did lie in them.

2. *See then that which may bring holiness into repute* and make us become proselytes to it. It casts a splendour upon us, and makes God number us among his jewels. Some are loath to embrace godliness for fear it will be a stain on their reputation, and bring them out of favour with great men. But you see how it raises a person's renown; it makes him precious in God's sight; he is a jewel. Believers, on account of their mystical union with Christ, have a preciousness above the angels: the angels are morning stars (*Job* 38:7). Believers are clothed with the sun of righteousness (*Rev.* 12:1).

3. *See the different opinion that God has of the godly and the wicked:* the one he esteems precious, the other vile. 'I will make thy grave; for thou art vile' (*Nahum* 1:14). This is spoken of King Sennacherib; though he was by birth noble, yet he was by sin vile. The Hebrew word for *vile* signifies *of base esteem*. Though the wicked are high in dignity and worldly grandeur, yet God slights them. A dunghill may be higher than other ground, but it sends forth noisome vapours: 'They are all together become filthy' (*Psa.* 14:3). In the original it is, 'They are become stinking.'

The wicked are compared to dogs and swine (2 *Pet.* 2:22) and to dross (*Ezek.* 22:19). Dross is the filth of the metal. Sinners are compared to chaff (*Psa.* 1:4). When a wicked man dies, there is only a little chaff blown away. A sinner is the most contemptible thing in nature; there is no worth in him while he lives and no loss of him when he dies.

A sinner is worse than a toad or serpent; a toad has nothing but what God has put into it, but a wicked man has that which the devil has put into him: 'Why hath Satan filled thine heart to lie to the Holy Ghost?' (*Acts* 5:3).

4. *See what a high estimate we should set upon the godly;* they are jewels, they are the glory of the creation. They are compared to stars for their beauty (*Rev.* 1:20), to spice trees for their perfume (*Song of Sol.* 4:14). They are the chariots and horsemen of Israel (2 *Kings* 2:12); they are the excellent of the earth (*Psa.* 16:3). The Lord would soon break up house in the world, but that he has some jewels in it.

Prize the saints though they are humbled with poverty. We esteem a pearl, though it lies in the dust. John the Baptist was girt with a leather girdle, yet he was a jewel (*Matt.* 11:9). He was the morning star to usher in the Sun of righteousness into the world. The saints are precious, for they are God's lesser heaven (*Isa.* 57:15).

5. *See the saints' safety:* they are God's jewels, and he will have a care to preserve them. A man is careful that he does not lose his jewels. God often gives his people a temporal salvation. If a storm comes he knows how to hide his jewels. He hid a hundred prophets in a cave (*1 Kings* 18:4). The angel is commanded, before he poured his vial of curses on the earth, to seal the saints of God on their foreheads (*Rev.* 7:3), which was *signum salutare,* a mark of safety. However God will look to the spiritual safety of his jewels: 'None of them is lost' (*John* 17:12).

6. If the saints are God's jewels, then *how incensed and enraged will God be against those who shall abuse these*

jewels? Theodosius[1] counted them traitors who abused his statue. What will become of those who persecute God's saints, and tread upon his jewels? It goes near to God to see his jewels sprinkled with blood. What is done to them the Lord takes as done to himself: 'Why persecutest thou me?' (*Acts* 9:4). When the foot was trod on, the head cried out. The saints are God's royal diadem (*Isa.* 62:3). Will a king endure to have his robes spat upon, or his crown-royal thrown in the dust? 'He reproved kings for their sakes' (*Psa.* 105:14).

What monuments of God's vengeance were Nero, Diocletian, Gardiner,[2] and the rest of that persecuting tribe? 'Shall not God avenge his own elect? . . . I tell you that he will avenge them speedily' (*Luke* 18:7–8). Persecutors stand in the place where all God's arrows fly: 'He ordaineth his arrows against the persecutors' (*Psa.* 7:13). That is a killing Scripture: 'And this shall be the plague wherewith the LORD will smite all the people that have fought against Jerusalem; their flesh shall consume away while they stand upon their feet, and their eyes shall consume away in their holes, and their tongues shall consume away in their mouth' (*Zech.* 14:12).

SECOND USE: *Consolation.*

Here is comfort to the people of God, in case of the world's disesteem of them: God yet values them as jewels; and his judgment is according to truth (*Rom* 2:2). The

---

[1] Theodosius (c. AD 346–395), Roman emperor.

[2] Nero (AD 37–68), Roman emperor; Diocletian (AD 245–313), Roman emperor; Stephen Gardiner (c. 1493–1555), Bishop of Winchester under Henry VIII, a persecutor of Protestants.

wicked have low thoughts of the righteous. They beat down the price of these jewels as far as they can. They think them but refuse, flakes, and scales. They disdain them, load them with slanders and invectives. The prophet Elijah was looked upon by Ahab as the 'troubler of Israel' (*1 Kings* 18:17), and Luther was called a 'trumpet of rebellion'. St Paul was judged 'a pestilent fellow' (*Acts* 24:5). The wicked think that of all things in the world the saints may be best avoided: 'We are made as the filth of the world . . . the off-scouring of all things' (*1 Cor.* 4:13).

But this is *vinum in pectore,* a great consolation to believers that, low as is the esteem the reprobate world has of them, yet God has high thoughts of them; he numbers them among his jewels. They are compared for their preciousness to gold and silver (*Rev.* 1:20). They are the coins and medals that bear God's own image. They are princes in all lands (*Psa.* 45:16). Christ engraves their names on his breast, as the names of the twelve tribes were set with precious stones in gold upon Aaron's breastplate. God will give whole kingdoms to ransom his jewels (*Isa.* 43:3). The wicked think the godly are not worthy to live in the world (*Acts* 22:22) and God thinks the world is not worthy of them (*Heb.* 11:38). Hence it is that God takes away his jewels so fast, and places them among the cherubims.

THIRD USE: *Exhortation.*

1. *To the people of God.* Are you God's jewels? Then I beseech you to *shine as jewels.* Walk circumspectly

(ἀκριβῶς, 'accurately'), and holily: 'Among whom ye shine as lights in the world' (*Phil.* 2:15). Such as are God's jewels should let the world see they have worth in them. O Christians, let your lives be an imitation of the life of Christ. Such a jewel was Mr Bradford, the martyr, so humble and innocent in his demeanour that, at his death, many of the Papists could not refrain from weeping.[1]

Are you God's jewels? Do nothing that may eclipse or sully your lustre. When professors are proud, envious or censorious, when they break their promises, or cheat their creditors, these do not look like saints. What will others say? These are the devil's lumber, not God's jewels. Oh, I beseech you who profess to be of an higher rank than others, honour that worthy name by which you are called; shine as earthly angels: 'But ye are . . . a royal priesthood, . . . a peculiar people; that ye should shew forth the praises of him who hath called you' (*1 Pet.* 2:9). Alexander would have the Grecians known not only by their garments, but their virtues. God's people should be known by the sparkling of their graces. Shall there be no difference in behaviour between the wicked and the godly, between a clod of earth and a diamond? Let it appear that you are candidates for heaven. You who are God's people, the Lord expects some singular thing from you (*Matt.* 5:47). He looks that you should bring more glory to him and by your exemplary piety make proselytes to religion.

2. The godly should be *thankful*. God has taken you out of the rubbish of mankind, and made you jewels: 'He raiseth up the poor out of the dust' (*Psa.* 113:7), that he

[1] John Bradford (1510–55) burnt at the stake in Mary Tudor's reign.

may set him with princes. So God has raised you out of the dust of a natural estate, and ennobled you, that he may set you with angels, those princes above. Oh, admire God! Set the crown of your praises upon the head of free grace. A gratulatory, thankful frame of heart is pleasing to God. If repentance is the joy, praise is the music of heaven. Bless God who has wrought such a change in you and, of lumps of earth and sin, has made you jewels.

3. *There is a time shortly coming when God will make up his jewels;* 'In that day when I make up my jewels'.

QUESTION 1: *What is meant by God's making up his jewels?*

ANSWER: There is a difference between God's *making* of jewels, and his *making up* of jewels. God's making of jewels is when he works grace, but what is God's making up of jewels? This implies two things.

Firstly, *God's gathering his saints together.* God's *making up* his jewels implies his gathering his saints together. The godly in this life are like scattered pearls, they lie distant one from another, and are dispersed into several regions; but there is a day coming when God will gather all his saints together, as one puts all his pearls together on a string. There must be such an aggregation or gathering together of God's scattered saints:

i. *From the near relation they have to all the Persons in the Trinity.* God the Father has chosen these jewels and set them apart for himself (*Psa.* 4:3), and will he lose any of his elect? They are related to Christ. He has bought these jewels with his blood, and will he lose his purchase? They are related to the Holy Spirit. He has sanctified them. When they were a lump of sin, he made them jewels; and when he has bestowed cost on them, will he lose his cost? Will he not string these pearls, and put them in his celestial cabinet?

ii. *There must be a gathering together of God's scattered saints from the prayer of Christ.* It was Christ's prayer to his Father, that he would make up his jewels, that he would gather together his pearls, that they might be with him in heaven: 'That they . . . be with me where I am' (*John* 17:24). Christ will not be content till all the elect jewels lie together in his bosom. He does not think himself complete till all his saints be with him.

USE: Here is *a sovereign comfort* to the people of God in two cases.

1. In case of *scattering*. God's people are scattered up and down in the world; and, which is worst, these jewels lie among rubbish, they dwell among the wicked: 'Woe is me that I dwell in the tents of Kedar' (*Psa.* 120:5). Kedar was Ishmael's son. 'Woe is me', says David, 'that I live with an Ishmael-brood.' The wicked are still molesting the righteous. God's jewels lie scattered among the unclean. But here is the comfort, that shortly God will gather his people from among the wicked, he will make up his jewels, and all the pearls and precious stones shall be by themselves in bliss.

2. It is comfort in case of *dividing*. God's people here are divided; their love is so little it may almost lie upon a knife's point. They often look suspiciously upon one

another. These divisions are unseemly and are flaws in God's diamonds. Discord among Christians brings a reproach upon religion, advances Satan's kingdom, and hinders the growth of grace. Divisions are fatal, and do presage God's judgments coming upon us.

But this is comfort, God will shortly make up his jewels: he will so gather his saints together that he will unite them together. They shall be all of one heart (*Acts* 2:46). What a happy time it will be when the saints shall be as so many pearls upon one string, and shall accord together in a blessed unity!

Secondly, God's making up his jewels also implies *his perfecting his saints*. A thing is said to be made up when it is perfected. You make up a garment when you perfect it. You make up a watch when you put all the wheels and pins in perfect order. So God's making up his jewels signifies his perfecting them. The godly in this life are imperfect. They cast but a faint lustre of holiness, they receive but 'the firstfruits of the Spirit' (*Rom.* 8:23), that is, a small measure of grace: the first fruits under the law were but a handful compared to the whole vintage.

The consideration of this may humble us if we are jewels, yet imperfect. Our knowledge is chequered with ignorance (*1 Cor* 13:5). Our love to God is feeble. Behold here clouds in the diamond. This may take down our topsail of pride, to consider how incomplete we are. But when God shall make up his jewels, and perfect his saints, it will be a glorious time; and this brings me to the second question.

QUESTION 2: *What is that day when God will make up his jewels?*

ANSWER: Firstly, God makes up his jewels *at the day of death*. Then he makes the saints' graces perfect. For this reason the saints departed are called 'the spirits of just men made perfect (*Heb.* 12:23). Sin so mixes with and dwells within a Christian that he cannot write a copy of holiness without blotting it. Grace, though it abates, yet it does not abolish corruption. But at death God makes up his jewels; he perfects the graces of his people. Will not that be a blessed time, never to have a vain thought again, never to be within the sight of a temptation or the fear of a relapse?

This, I think, may make death desirable to the godly; then the Lord will make up his jewels, he will complete the graces of his children; they shall be as holy as they desire to be, and as God would have them to be. How will God's diamonds sparkle when they shall be without flaws? In that day of death when God makes up his jewels, the saints' light will be clear, and their love will be perfect.

Their light will be clear. They shall be so divinely irradiated, that they shall know the 'deep things of God'. They shall in this sense be 'as the angels' (*Matt.* 22:30). Their faculty of thought shall be raised higher and made more capacious than in innocency. Through the crystal glass of Christ's human nature, the saints shall have glorious transparent sights of God: they shall know as they are known (*1 Cor.* 13:12); a riddle too mysterious for us mortals, if not for angels, to expound.

In that day the saints' love will be perfect. Love is the queen of the graces, it outlives all the other graces. In this life our love to God is lukewarm and sometimes frozen. A believer weeps that he can love God no more: but at the day of death when God makes up his jewels, then the saints' love shall be seraphic. The spark of love shall be blown up into a pure flame: the saints shall love God *secundum actum*, as the Schoolmen say, as much as they are able. They shall love him superlatively and without defect; they shall be made up of love. Oh, blessed day of death! When God shall make up his jewels, the saints' graces shall shine forth in their meridian splendour.

Secondly, God makes up his jewels *at the day of the resurrection.* Then he makes the saints bodies perfect. These, like sparkling diamonds, shall shine in glory. At the resurrection God is said to *change* the bodies of the saints (*Phil.* 3:21). How will he change them? Not that they shall be other bodies than they were before. The substance of their bodies shall not be changed, but the qualities. As wool, when it is dyed into a purple colour, is not altered in the *substance*, but in the *quality*, and is made more illustrious, so God in making up his jewels will cause a greater resplendency in the saints' bodies than before.

When God makes up the jewels of the saints' bodies at the resurrection, they shall be perfect in four ways.

i. *In amiability or sweetness of beauty.* Here the bodies of the righteous are often deformed. Leah has her weak eyes, and Barzillai his lameness; but at the resurrection the bodies of the saints shall be of unspotted fairness:

and no wonder, for they shall be made like Christ's glorious body (*Phil* 3:21).

ii. When God at the resurrection makes up the jewels of the saints' bodies, *they shall have perfection of parts.* Their bodies in this world may be maimed and dismembered; but in the day of the resurrection they shall have all the parts of their bodies restored (*Acts* 3:21). Such as have lost an eye, shall have their eye again; such as lack a leg or an arm, shall have their arm again.

iii. When God makes up the jewels of the saints' bodies at the resurrection, *they shall be swift and lively in their motion.* Here the bodies of the saints move heavily, but then they shall be sprightly, and move rapidly from one place to another. Here the body is a weight; in heaven it shall be a wing.

iv. When God makes up the jewels of the saints' bodies, *they shall be immortal.* The body once glorified shall never be subject to death: 'This corruptible must put on incorruption' (*1 Cor.* 15:53). Heaven is a healthy climate; no passing-bell[1] goes there. This mortal shall put on immortality.

Let us labour to be in the number of God's jewels, that when the Lord shall make up his jewels, he may perfect our souls and bodies in glory.

QUESTION: How shall we know that we are in the number of God's jewels?

ANSWER: Have we inherent holiness? 'But ye are washed, but ye are sanctified' (*1 Cor.* 6:11). We are not

---

[1] Bell tolled at a person's death or funeral.

jewels by creation, but regeneration. If holiness sparkles in us, it is a sign we are jewels; and then when God comes to make up his jewels, he will put glory upon our souls and bodies forever.

14

GOD REWARDS HIS PEOPLE BY SPARING THEM

The third part of the saints' reward is God's sparing them: 'I will spare them as a man spareth his own son that serveth him.' The Hebrew word to spare signifies to use clemency: in this phrase is a *meiosis*,[1] there is less said and more intended. 'I will spare them', that is, 'I will deal with them as a father does with his son. The kind of tenderness that a father shows to his child, the same will I show to those that fear me.'

DOCTRINE: God will deal with them that fear him as a father does with his son.

Two things are in this proposition:

1. *That God is a Father*. He is a father by creation. He has given us our being: 'Have not we all one father? Hath not one God created us?' (*Mal.* 2:10). God is also a father by election: he has culled out a certain number to be his children (*Eph.* 1:4). And God is a father by special grace: he stamps his impress of holiness upon men (*Col.* 3:10). All God's children resemble him, though some are more like him than others.

---

[1] Understatement (Greek, diminution).

2. *That God will deal with those that fear him as a father does with his son.*

i. God will accept them as a father does his son. If the child only lisps and can hardly speak plainly, the father takes all in good part. So God, as a father, will accept what his children do in sincerity: 'There will I require your offerings . . . I will accept you with your sweet savour' (*Ezek.* 20:40–41).

ii. To such as fear God, he will be full of bowels[1] to them as a father is to his son. There are in God bowels of compassion and bowels of complacency.

Bowels of compassion. A father feels for his child. Sozomen[2] makes mention of a father who offered to be put to death for his two sons who were sentenced to die. God has soundings of bowels (*Isa.* 63:15). The compassions of parents are steel and marble compared with God's, 'the tender mercy of our God' (*Luke* 1:78). In the Greek it is 'the bowels of mercy'. These bowels make God sympathize with his children in misery. He is touched in their wounds: 'As a father pitieth his children so the LORD pitieth them that fear him' (*Psa.* 103:13).

In God are also *bowels of complacency.* How dearly did Jacob love Benjamin! His life was bound up in him (*Gen.* 44:30). All the affections of parents come from God. They are but a drop of his ocean, a spark of his flame. God's love is a love that 'passeth knowledge' (*Eph.*

---

[1] Pity, tenderness. The emotions were spoken of as if seated in the bowels.

[2] Sozomen, fifth-century church historian originally from Bethelia, near Gaza in Palestine.

3:19). The saints cannot love their own souls so entirely as God loves them. In particular,

a. God loves the persons of his children; they are the apple of his eye (*Zech.* 2:8). He engraves them upon the palms of his hands (*Isa.* 49:16). This alludes to those who carry about them, graven on the stone of their ring, the picture of some dear friend whom they entirely love.

b. God loves the places his children were born in the better for their sakes: 'God loveth the gates of Zion' (*Psa.* 87:2); 'This and that man was born in her' (verse 5); that is, 'this and that believer'. God loves the very ground his children go upon. Why was Judea, the ancient seat of Israel, called 'a delightsome land' (*Mal.* 3:12)? Not so much delightful for the fruit growing in it, as for the saints living in it.

c. God so loves his children that he charges the great ones of the world upon pain of death not to hurt them. Their persons are sacred. 'He reproved kings for their sakes; saying, Touch not mine anointed' (*Psa.* 105:14–15). By 'anointed' are meant such as have the anointing of the Spirit (*1 John* 2:20).

d. God delights in his children's company, he loves to see their faces, 'Let me see thy countenance' (*Song of Sol.* 2:14). If but two or three of God's children meet and pray together, God will be sure to make one of the company: 'There am I in the midst of them' (*Matt.* 18:20).

e. God so loves his children that his eye is never off them: 'The eye of the LORD is upon them that fear him' (*Psa.* 33:18). But is this such a privilege, to have God's eye upon his children? God's eye is upon the wicked too.

Answer: It is one kind of eye that the judge casts upon the malefactor, and another that the prince casts upon his favourite. God's eye upon the wicked is an eye of revenge, but his eye upon his children is an eye of benediction.

f. God sets a continual guard about his children to preserve them from danger. He hides them in his pavilion (*Psa.* 27:5). He covers them with the golden feathers of his protection (*Psa.* 91:4). God preserved Athanasius[1] strangely; he put it into his mind to depart out of the house he was in the night before the enemies came to search for him. No prince goes so well guarded as God's child, for he has a guard of angels about him. The angels are a numerous guard: 'The mountain was full of horses and chariots of fire' (2 *Kings* 6:17). Those horses and chariots of fire were the angels of God, gathered in the manner of a huge host to defend the prophet Elijah.

g. God clothes his children in rich garments: 'Her clothing is of wrought gold' (*Psa.* 45:13). Jacob loved his son Joseph and gave him a finer coat to wear than the rest of his brethren: 'He made him a coat of many colours' (*Gen.* 37:3). God loves his children and gives them a finer coat, more curiously woven, a coat of diverse colours. It is partly made of Christ's righteousness, and partly of inherent holiness (*Rev.* 19:8).

h. Such is God's love that he thinks nothing too good for his children: he enriches them with the upper and lower springs; he gives them the finest of the wheat, and

---

[1] Athanasius (c. AD 296–373), theologian and writer of devout faith who championed Christian orthodoxy against Arianism.

honey out of the rock; he makes them a feast of fat things (*Isa.* 25:6). He gives them the body and blood of his Son, and delights to see his children spreading themselves as olive plants round about his table (*Psa.* 128:3).

iii. God will receive the petitions of such as are fearers of God as a father does his son's petitions. They may come boldly to the throne of grace (*Heb.* 4:16). If they come for pardon of sin, or strength against temptation, God will not deny them. Three things may cause boldness in prayer; the saints have a Father to pray to, the Spirit to help them to pray, and Jesus Christ as their Advocate to present their prayers.

iv. On such as are fearers of God, God will bestow an inheritance, as a father does upon his son. This inheritance is no less than a kingdom (*Luke* 12:32). In it are gates of pearl, rivers of pleasure; and (which is to be noted as a difference between God's settling an inheritance on his children, and an earthly father's settling an inheritance): a son cannot enjoy the inheritance till his father is dead; but every adopted child of God may at once enjoy both the inheritance and the father, because God is both father and inheritance (*Gen.* 15).

v. With such as are fearers of God, God will pass by many infirmities. That is what is meant by this expression in the text, 'I will spare them as a man spareth his own son.' What a wonder this is, that God did not spare the angels (2 *Pet.* 2:4)! No, he did not spare his natural Son (*Rom.* 8:32). Yet he will spare his adopted sons: '*I will spare them,* I will not use extremity as I might, but pass by many aberrations.'

CAUTION: It is not that the sins of God's children are hid from him, but such is his paternal clemency that he is pleased to bear with many frailties in his children. He spares them as a father spares his son. How often do God's people grieve his Spirit by the neglect of spiritual watchfulness, the loss of their first love; but God spares them! Israel provoked God with their murmurings, but he used fatherly indulgence towards them (*Psa.* 78:38; *Neh.* 9:17).

FIRST USE: *Information.*

1. From this word, 'I will spare them as a man spares his son', take notice that *the best need sparing.* 'If thou, LORD, shouldest mark iniquities, O Lord, who shall stand?' (*Psa.* 130:3). The Papists speak of merits, but how can we merit when our best services are so defective that we need sparing? How can these two stand together, our meriting and God's sparing? What will become of us without sparing mercy? We need to pray as Nehemiah, 'Remember me, O my God, concerning this also, and spare me according to the greatness of thy mercy' (*Neh.* 13:22). Let us fly to this asylum, 'Lord, spare us as a father spares his son.'

2. See *God's different dealing with the godly and the wicked.* The Lord will not spare the wicked: 'I will not pity, nor spare, nor have mercy, but destroy them' (*Jer.* 13:14). It is sad when the prisoner begs of the judge to spare him, but the judge will show him no favour. God's

cup of wrath is unmixed (*Rev.* 14:10). Yet it is said to be mixed. The cup of wrath God gives the wicked is mixed with all sorts of plagues, but in this sense it is unmixed, without the least drop of mercy in it (*Psa.* 78:45–51). God for a while reprieves men, but forbearance is not forgiveness. Though God spare his children, yet obdurate sinners shall feel the weight of his wrath.

3. If the Lord spares his people as a father does his son, then *they should serve him as a son does his father*.

i. They should serve him *willingly*: 'Know thou the God of thy father, and serve him with a willing mind' (*1 Chron.* 28:9). God does not love to be put to strain. Cain's sacrifice was rejected because he brought it grudgingly and against his mind. It was rather the paying of a tax than a free-will offering. The best obedience is what is voluntary, as that is the best honey which drops from the comb. God sometimes accepts of willingness without the work (*1 Kings* 8:18), but never of the work without willingness.

ii. They should serve God *universally*. True obedience is uniform; it observes one command as well as another; it fulfils duties difficult and dangerous. As the needle points the way that the magnet draws, so a gracious heart inclines to those things which the word suggests (*Luke* 1:6). It is the note of a hypocrite to be discriminating in obedience; some sin he will indulge (*2 Kings* 5:18), some duty he will dispense with; his obedience is lame on one foot.

iii. *They should serve God swiftly*. Beware of a dull temper of soul; the loveliness of obedience is in the liveliness. We read of two women, 'The wind was in their wings' (*Zech.* 5:9). Wings are swift, but wind in the wings denotes great swiftness. Such swiftness should be in our obedience to God. If God spares us as a father does his son, we should serve him as a son does his father.

SECOND USE: *Exhortation.*

If God spares us as a father does his son, *let us imitate God*. It is natural for children to imitate their parents; what the father does, the child is apt to learn the same. Let us imitate God in this one thing: As God spares us, and passes by many failures, so let us be sparing in our censures of others; let us look upon the weaknesses and indiscretions of our brethren with a more tender compassionate eye.

Indeed, in cases of scandal we ought not to bear with others, but sharply reprove them. But if through inadvertency or passion they act wrongly, let us pity and pray for them. How much God bears with us! He spares us, and shall not we be sparing to others? Perhaps they may be wronged, and false things may be said to their charge. Athanasius was falsely accused by the Arians of adultery, Basil[1] of heresy. It is usual for the world to misrepresent the people of God; therefore let us be sparing in our censures. God spares us, and shall not we be sparing towards others?

THIRD USE: *Comfort.*

Here is comfort to the children of God in case of failings. The Lord will not be severe to mark what they have done amiss, but will spare them. He passes by many infirmities: 'He will rest in his love' (*Zeph.* 3:17); in the original it is, 'He will *be silent* in his love', as if the prophet had said, though the church had her failings, yet God's love was such, that it would not suffer him to mention them. God turns a blind eye to many oversights: 'Mine eye spared them from destroying them' (*Ezek.* 20:17). I speak not of presumptuous sins, but of failings such as vain thoughts, deadness in duty, sudden surprises by temptation: these being mourned for, God for Christ's sake will spare us as a father does his son.

This is one of the richest comforts in the Book of God. Who is he that lives and sins not? How defective we are in our best duties! How full our lives are either of blanks or of blots! Were it not for sparing mercy, we should all go to hell. But this text is a standing cordial; if our hearts are sincere, God will spare us as a father does his son: 'I will not execute the fierceness of mine anger' (*Hos.* 11:9).

I know not a greater rock of support for a fainting Christian than this; God will abate the severity of the law; though we come short in our duty, he will not fail of his mercy, but will spare us as a father spares his son.

15

THE RIGHTEOUS AND
THE WICKED DISCERNED

Then shall ye return, and discern between the righteous and the wicked, between him that serveth God, and him that serveth him not (Mal. 3:18).

Here follows the close of the chapter, which I shall little more than paraphrase. These words are spoken to the wicked, as Piscator,[1] Calvin, Grotius, and other learned expositors assert; for though the godly shall at last discern what a difference God makes between them and the wicked, how indulgent he is to the one, and how severe to the other, yet this text is chiefly spoken to the wicked: 'Ye have said, It is vain to serve God' (verse 14); and 'Now we call the proud happy; yea, they that work wickedness are set up' (verse 15). Well, says God, though now you call the proud happy and the godly indiscreet, yet when I have made up my jewels, then you wicked ones shall see clearly what a difference I make between the righteous, and the wicked, between him that serves God and him that does not serve him. Then, when it is too late,

---

[1] Johannes Piscator (1546–1625), German Reformed theologian and commentator.

when the day of grace is past, and the drawbridge of mercy is pulled up, then shall you discern a difference between the holy and the profane.

DOCTRINE 1: *The wicked at present have their eyes shut;* 'The LORD hath not given you an heart to perceive, and eyes to see, and ears to hear, unto this day' (*Deut.* 29:4). Natural men have the sword upon their right eye (*Zech* 11:17). They see no difference between the pious and the impious; they cannot see but that it fares as well with the wicked as the righteous; nay, it seems to fare better. The wicked flourish: 'These are the ungodly, who prosper in the world; they increase in riches' (*Psa.* 73:12); whereas those that pray and fast are oppressed. The wicked bless themselves, and think they are now in a better condition than the righteous; the matter is not to be wondered at, for 'the God of this world hath blinded the minds of' sinners (2 *Cor.* 4:4). But at last their eyes shall be opened; and that brings me to the second doctrine.

DOCTRINE 2: *There is a time shortly coming when impious, grossly wicked sinners shall see an obvious difference between the godly and the wicked.* The tables will then be turned: 'Then shall ye return, and discern between the righteous and the wicked.'

QUESTION: When is the time when the eyes of sinners shall be opened, and they shall see a difference between the righteous and the wicked?

ANSWER: There are two times when sinners shall see a manifest difference between the righteous and the wicked.

Firstly, *at the day of judgment*. That will be a day of discrimination. Things will then appear in their proper colours; the difference will easily be seen between good and bad; the one being absolved, the other condemned.

Secondly, *at the hour of separation*, when God shall eternally separate the reprobate from the elect, as a fan separates the chaff from the wheat, and there shall be a visible discerning between the righteous and wicked. 'Before him shall be gathered all nations: and he shall separate them one from another, as a shepherd divideth his sheep from the goats' (*Matt.* 25:32). Jesus Christ will take his saints up with him into glory, and will cast the wicked down to hell. He will make up the godly as jewels, and make up the wicked in bundles: 'Bind them in bundles to burn them' (*Matt.* 13:30). Now sinners shall be convinced with a vengeance, that the state of the righteous and the wicked is different: they shall see the righteous advanced to a kingdom, and themselves cast into a fiery prison.

Oh, the dreadfulness of that place of torment! Could men lay their ears to the infernal lake, and but for one hour hear the groans and shrieks of the damned, they would tell us that they now *see* what before they would not *believe*, the infinite difference between the righteous and the wicked. In hell is torment upon torment, 'blackness of darkness' (*Jude* 13), 'chains of darkness' (2 *Pet.* 2:4). These chains are God's decree ordaining, and his power binding men under wrath; and that which accentuates and puts a sting into the torments of the wicked is that they shall be always scorching in the torrid zone of

God's wrath: 'The smoke of their torment ascendeth up for ever and ever' (*Rev.* 14:11). Christ said of his suffering on the cross, 'It is finished'; but sinners shall never say of their sufferings in hell, they are finished. No, if the damned had lain in hell as many thousand years as there are drops in the sea, eternity has yet to begin.

First Use: *Information.*

This may inform all wicked men that, no matter how blind they are now, yet at last the veil shall be taken from their eyes. They now count themselves the only happy men, and look upon the people of God with derision. They load them with invectives and curse them with their excommunications. Well, the time is not far off when the wicked shall clearly discern who belong to Christ, and who belong to the devil. As Moses said to Korah and his company, 'Tomorrow the Lord will shew who are his' (*Num.* 16:5), so at the day of judgment the Lord will show who are his, and who are not; nay, sooner than that: at the day of death the wicked shall guess how it is like to be with them for eternity.

Oh, that the eyes of sinners may be speedily opened, that they may in time see the difference of things, the beauty that is in holiness, and the astonishing madness that is in sin.

Second Use: *Consolation to the righteous.* Though at present they are slighted, and have the odium of the world cast upon them, yet shortly God will make a visible difference between them and the wicked; as it was with Pharaoh's two officers, the butler and the baker; at first there seemed to be no difference between them, but in a short while there was difference made. The chief butler was advanced to honour, but the chief baker was executed (*Gen.* 40:21–22). So though now God's people are low and despised, and the wicked treat them with boastful insolence, yet when the critical day comes, there shall be a final separation made between the righteous and the wicked. The one shall be dignified, the other damned (*Matt.* 25:46).

Be encouraged therefore, saints of God, to persist in a course of holiness. Though now you seem to be lowermost, yet in the resurrection you shall be uppermost: 'The upright shall have dominion over them in the morning' (*Psa.* 49:14); they shall have dominion over the wicked in the morning of the resurrection. They shall then laugh the wicked to scorn (*Psa.* 52:6). Then shall the difference be seen between the righteous and the wicked, between him that served God and him that served him not.

16

A CONSOLATION IN AFFLICTION

Thou hast dealt well with thy servant, O LORD
(Psa. 119:65).

The Psalms are the marrow of the Bible. They are both for *delight* and *use*, like rich cordials which not only gratify the palate but strengthen the spirits. This Psalm is full of divine and spiritual matter. It was composed, if not sung, by the sweet singer of Israel. The words fall into two parts.

1. *God's kindness to David:* He dealt well with him.

2. *David's grateful acknowledgment of this favour:* 'Thou hast dealt well with thy servant, O LORD.'

From God's kindness to David, observe:

DOCTRINE: *That God deals well with his people.* 'God hath dealt graciously with me' (*Gen.* 33.11). God's people often fail to respond to his love; but though they deal badly with God, God deals well with them.

God's dealing well with his people arises from the intrinsic goodness of his nature. 'God is love' (*1 John* 4:16). From this flow all acts of royal bounty.

QUESTION: In what ways does God's dealing well with his people appear?

ANSWER: In enriching them with varied mercies; his paths 'drop fatness' (*Psa.* 65:11); he feeds, adopts, crowns them; and is not this dealing well with them?

OBJECTION: But how does God deal well with the saints when he lays his hand so heavy upon them in affliction? His pen is full of gall, and he writes bitter things against them: 'All the day long have I been plagued, and chastened every morning' (*Psa.* 73:14). How does God deal *well* with his people when it fares *ill* with them?

ANSWER: It must be held as an undoubted maxim that when the Lord severely chastises the saints he deals well with them, but we are ready to question this truth, and say as the virgin Mary to the angel, 'How can this be?' Therefore I shall demonstrate it, that, when it goes badly with the righteous, yet God deals well with them.

1. When the Lord afflicts the saints yet he deals well with them, *because he is their God*. David was in the depths of sorrow (*Psa.* 130:1), yet he could say the Lord was his portion (*Psa.* 16:5). God is an 'exceeding great reward' (*Gen.* 15:1). He is a whole paradise of delight, the good in which all good is contained. He who has God for his God, all his estate lies in jewels. If then God passes

over himself to his people by a deed of gift to be their God, here is enough to compensate for all their troubles. What can God give more than himself?

2. When it goes badly with the godly, yet God deals well with them *because, while he is inflicting evil upon them, he is doing them good.* That which the text renders, 'Thou hast dealt well with thy servant', in the Hebrew reads, 'Thou hast done good to thy servant.' 'It is good for me that I have been afflicted' (*Psa.* 119:71): David does not say, 'It is good for me that I have been in prosperity', but 'that I have been afflicted'. God does his people good by affliction in two ways:

i. *The godly grow wiser.* Affliction is a school of light. *Vexatio dat intellectum* (trouble gives understanding). It discovers pride, earthliness, unmortified passion, which they could not have believed was in their hearts. 'If they be . . . holden in cords of affliction, then he sheweth them . . . their transgressions' (*Job* 36:8–9). Affliction cures the eyesight.

ii. *Affliction promotes holiness.* The more the diamond is cut, the more it sparkles: 'That we might be partakers of his holiness' (*Heb.* 12:10). When prosperity makes grace rust, God scours us with affliction. The godly are thankful for their sufferings. God by the wholesome discipline of the cross makes them more humble, more conformed to Christ's image. The sharp frosts of affliction bring on the spring flowers of grace. Now if God, while he is chastising, is doing us good, then surely he deals well with us.

3. When God puts his children to the school of the cross, yet he deals well with them *because he does not leave them without a promise:* 'God is faithful, who will not suffer you to be tempted above that ye are able' (*1 Cor.* 10:13). God knows our frame, that we are feeble and weak; our flesh is not 'of brass' (*Job* 6:12). And the Lord will not try us above our strength, he will not lay a giant's burden upon a child's back. God will not stretch the strings of his violin too hard, lest they break. If God should strike with one hand, he will support with the other (*Song of Sol.* 8:3). Either he will make our yoke lighter, or our faith stronger. This promise is honey at the end of the rod.

4. God deals well with his people when he afflicts *because afflictions are preventative.*

i. *They prevent sin:* 'Lest I should be exalted above measure . . . there was given to me a thorn in the flesh' (*2 Cor.* 12:7). Prosperity, like opium, is ready to make men fall asleep in sin. God awakens them by the voice of the rod, and so prevents a spiritual lethargy.

ii. *They prevent hell:* 'We are chastened of the Lord, that we should not be condemned with the world' (*1 Cor.* 11:32). Does not a judge deal well with a prisoner when he lays some light penalty on him and saves his life? Is it not goodness in God, when he lays upon us light afflic- tion, and saves us from wrath to come (*2 Cor.* 4:17)? What is a drop of sorrow which the godly taste compared to the bottomless sea of wrath the wicked must drink?

5. When God corrects he deals well with his people *because all he does is in love.* Afflictions are, as Gregory Nazianzen says, sharp arrows, but they are shot from the hand of a loving father. As God's not afflicting the wicked is in anger, so God's hand is heaviest when it is lightest: 'I will not punish your daughters when they commit whoredom' (*Hos.* 4:14). A father gives over correcting a child whom he intends to disinherit; so God's chastising the godly is in love. 'As many as I love, I rebuke' (*Rev.* 3:19). When God has the look of an enemy, he has the heart of a father. As when Abraham lifts up his hand to sacrifice Isaac, he loved him; so when God sacrifices the comforts of his children, he loves them. Was not God severe against Christ? Yet it was proclaimed by a voice from heaven, 'This is my beloved Son' (*Matt.* 3:17). Well then, if God only sends love tokens to us, he deals well with us.

6. God deals well with his people when he afflicts them *because he moderates his stroke;* 'I will correct thee in measure' (*Jer.* 30:11; *Jer* 46:28). God does not smite his children as much as he might. He 'did not stir up all his wrath' (*Psa.* 78:38); God does not make the cup as bitter as he could. He uses lenitives[1] rather than corrosives.[2] He lays a lighter burden on when he might lay on a heavier. Does God take away a child? He might take away his Spirit. Does he chastise the body? He might torment the conscience. God does not correct his children as much as

---

[1] Soothing or gentle medications.
[2] Harsh substances applied to burn out lesions or growths

they have deserved: 'Thou . . . hast punished us less than our iniquities deserve' (*Ezra* 9:13). Does God make us drink a cup of wormwood? We have deserved to drink a cup of wrath. Does God cut us short? We have deserved he should cut us off. Do the waters of affliction come up to our ankles (see *Ezek.* 47:3)? We have deserved to be drowned in these waters.

7. When God afflicts his children he deals well with them *because he keeps them from sinning in affliction*: 'I pray . . . that thou shouldest keep them from the evil' (*John* 17:15).

i. *The godly are kept from impatience*. When the wicked are under God's black rod, they either faint or fret: 'Men were scorched with great heat, and blasphemed the name of God' (*Rev.* 16:9); but the godly are silent under the rod: 'And Aaron held his peace' (*Lev.* 10:3). It was a sore trial; both his sons were consumed with fire, but 'Aaron held his peace.' God's people open their ear to hear the voice of the rod, but shut their mouth; they have not one word to say against God.

ii. *The godly dare not use any dishonest means to extricate themselves out of trouble*. Wicked men, like criminals, do not care how they get loose; they will sin themselves out of their difficulties. The people of God would rather lie in the furnace to have their dross purged than come out too soon. They will not purchase the liberty of their persons by ensnaring their consciences. Does not God deal well with his children in keeping them from sinning in affliction? Affliction cannot do the mischief that sin does. One is like a rent in a garment, the other is like a rent in one's flesh. Affliction may deprive us of our estates, but sin deprives us of our God.

8. God deals well with his children in affliction *because though he correct them, he does not forsake them.* Indeed, 'Zion said, The LORD hath forsaken me' (*Isa.* 49:14), but that was under a temptation; 'For the Lord will not cast off for ever' (*Lam.* 3:31). God may alter his providence, not his purpose: he may change his dispensation, but not his disposition. 'How shall I give thee up, Ephraim?' (*Hos.* 11:8). It alludes to a father who is about to disinherit his son, but when he is going to set his hand to the deed, his heart begins to stir: 'I am his father, and though he is a rebellious son, yet he is a son; how shall I disinherit him?' Such is the working of God's heart towards his children; though he may give them a severe rebuke, yet he will not disinherit them from his mercy.

9. God deals well with his children in affliction *because, though their condition should be sad, yet it is not so bad as others.* The Lord puts a difference between the chastisements of the godly and the punishments of the wicked. The godly man has pain in his sickness, but the wicked man has 'wrath with his sickness' (*Eccles.* 5:17). The Lord shoots a single arrow at the godly, but a whole shower of arrows at the wicked; he punishes them in their body, estate, conscience. A good man has God to pity him in his sorrows (*Isa.* 63:9). But the wicked have God to

laugh at them in their mercies (*Prov.* 1:26). The godly have Christ to pray for them, in their afflictions; but the impenitent when in torment, are shut out of Christ's prayer: 'I pray not for the world' (*John* 17:9).

God's people are apt to say, never did any suffer as they; but it is worse with the wicked; their sins and sufferings meet together.

10. God in affliction deals well with his children *because, if he takes away one comfort, he leaves more behind*. God threatened Jerusalem that she would be stripped of all her jewels and left bare (*Ezek.* 16:39). But you who belong to God may 'sing of mercy and judgment' (*Psa.* 101:1). If God has fleeced your estate, he has raised you up friends. If he has taken away one of your jewels, he has left you more. If he has plucked one dear relation from you, he has left other sweet clusters behind, and can double your comfort in them. Is not all this kindness? But this is our sin, we grieve more for one loss than we are thankful for a hundred mercies. Jacob was more troubled for the loss of Joseph than he was comforted with the lives of all his other children (*Gen.* 37:35).

11. When God afflicts, he deals well with his people *because he takes away nothing from them but he gives them that which is better*. What damage can it be to a man to lose his farthings and have gold given him? If God takes away health he gives holiness. If he takes away a child he gives a Christ; is not this better? God takes away a flower and gives a jewel.

12. When God afflicts his children he deals well with them *because he affords them his divine presence:* 'I will be with him in trouble' (*Psa.* 91:15). God never promised us a charter of exemption from trouble, but he has promised to be with us in trouble. Better be in a prison and have God's presence, than on a throne and lack it. God's presence gives courage (*Acts* 23:11). When Polycarp was near the theatre and going to suffer, a voice came from heaven, 'Be of good cheer, O Polycarp.'[1] Was not Christ with the three children? Did he not go with them into the fire? 'I see four men loose, walking in the midst of the fire . . . and the form of the fourth is like the Son of God' (*Dan.* 3:25). He who is the Second Person in the Trinity made the fourth person in the furnace.

13. God in afflicting deals well with his children *because he gives them that which makes amends for their afflictions;* he drops in the oil of gladness; he makes them gather grapes of thorns: 'Your sorrow shall be turned into joy' (*John* 16:20). We see a godly man's sufferings but we know not what joy he feels, as we hear the roaring of the sea, but do not see the gold at the bottom. Philip the Landgrave of Hesse said that in his trouble he felt the divine consolations of the martyrs; here was honey out of the lion. The saints have been sometimes so sweetly enlarged that they would rather endure their afflictions than lack their comforts: 'As the sufferings of Christ abound in us, so our consolation also aboundeth by Christ' (2 *Cor.* 1:5). St Paul had his prison songs (*Acts*

---

[1] Polycarp (c. AD 70–156) Bishop of Smyrna and martyr.

16:25). This bird of paradise could sing in winter. God turns the waters of Marah into wine; he keeps his cordials for cases of fainting. When the saints taste most of the wrath of men, they shall feel most of the love of God. Thus the Lord candies his wormwood with sugar.

14. When God corrects his children he deals well with them *because these paroxysms or hot trials do not last long*. After the clouds, the sun. 'I will for this afflict the seed of David, but not for ever' (*1 Kings* 11:39). God will love forever, but not afflict forever; he will before long give his people a writ of ease. A sinner's best, and a saint's worst, are but short; affliction is called a cup (*Ezek.* 23:32). The wicked drink a sea of wrath; the godly sip only of the cup of affliction, and God will shortly say, 'Let this cup pass away from them.' 'Sorrow and sighing shall fly away' (*Isa.* 35:10). As affliction has a sting to torment, so it has a wing to fly.

15. When God puts his children to the school of the cross he deals well with them *because these afflictions lead them by the hand to heaven*. By the cross, we mount to heaven. 'Our light affliction . . . worketh for us a far more exceeding and eternal weight of glory' (*2 Cor.* 4:17). Upon the dark colour of affliction God lays the golden colour of glory. O weeping saint, what a blessed change you shall shortly have! You shall change your pilgrimage for paradise. You shall have your wish. Are riches desirable? You shall have gates of pearl. Is honour desirable? You shall have white robes. Is pleasure desirable? You

shall enter into the joy of the Lord. Oh, think what it will be to be sweetly immersed in the River of Life, and bathe in the honey streams of God's love for ever. Think what the beatifical vision will be: what it will be to wear a garland made of the flowers of paradise. Think what it will be to have the soul thicker set with jewels of glory than the firmament is bespangled with stars. Oh, what a compensation this will be for all a Christian's trials! A sight of this bliss will make him forget his sufferings. One sunbeam of glory will dry up the water of his tears.

Use of the Doctrine.

If God deals well with us when he chastises us, then it is fitting for us to cherish good thoughts of God. We are prone in adversity to think harshly of God; this arises from pride. Such commonly as are of high spirits are of high passions; they think themselves better than others, and that they have deserved better at God's hands; and now pride vents itself in murmuring. Oh, let us take heed of having harsh thoughts of God. The patient has no cause to think badly of the physician when he prescribes him a bitter potion, seeing it is in order to a cure. God's afflictive providences are the strokes of a father, not the wounds of an enemy. God smites that he may save. Out of the bitterest drug God distils his glory, and our happiness.

Let us think well of God; *nay, in all adverse providences let us learn to bless God.* 'In every thing give thanks' (1 *Thess.* 5:18). If in everything, then in affliction. And with good reason, because God deals well with us. Job blessed

God in affliction (*Job* 1:21). The smiting of Job's body was like striking upon a musical instrument: he sounded forth thankfulness. A gracious soul should bless God that he will take so much notice of him as to visit him with the rod (*Job* 7:18) and is so kind as rather to afflict him than lose him. This shows a high degree of grace, not only to justify God in affliction, but to magnify him. Believers are God's temples, and where should his praises be sounded forth but in his temples?